For Good Measure
A Diabetic Cookbook

For Good Measure
A Diabetic Cookbook

**Over 80 Healthy,
Flavorful Recipes to
Balance Blood Sugar**

JENNIFER SHUN

CORAL GABLES, FL

For permission requests, please contact the publisher at:

Mango Publishing Group

2850 S Douglas Road, 2nd Floor

Coral Gables, FL 33134 USA

info@mango.bz

For special orders, quantity sales, course adoptions and corporate sales, please email the publisher at sales@mango.bz. For trade and wholesale sales, please contact Ingram Publisher Services at customer.service@ingramcontent.com or +1.800.509.4887.

For Good Measure: A Diabetic Cookbook: Over 80 Healthy, Flavorful Recipes to Balance Blood Sugar

Library of Congress Cataloging-in-Publication number: 2023943713

ISBN: (hc) 978-1-68481-339-1 (pb) 978-1-68481-340-7 (e) 978-1-68481-341-4

BISAC category code: CKB025000, COOKING / Health & Healing / Diabetic & Sugar-Free

The information provided in this book is based on the research, insights, and experiences of the author. Every effort has been made to provide accurate and up-to-date information; however, neither the author nor the publisher warrants the information provided is free of factual error. This book is not intended to diagnose, treat, or cure any medical condition or disease, nor is it intended as a substitute for professional medical care. All matters regarding your health should be supervised by a qualified healthcare professional. The author and publisher disclaim all liability for any adverse effects arising out of or relating to the use or application of the information or advice provided in this book.

To you, Mia...and to everyone who has ever battled blood sugar.

CONTENTS

Breakfast

Salads

Soups

Sides

Mains

Snacks

Endings

Foreword

DR. CHERYL A. M. ANDERSON

Diabetes is a chronic health condition in which the body is unable to properly regulate blood glucose (sugar) levels, leading to high levels of glucose in the blood. There are two main types of diabetes: Type 1 Diabetes which is typically diagnosed in childhood and is caused by the body's immune system attacking the cells in the pancreas that produce insulin, and Type 2 Diabetes which is more commonly diagnosed in adults and is often related to lifestyle factors such as not eating healthfully, physical inactivity, and body weight.

According to the World Health Organization, diabetes is one of the leading causes of death worldwide, and the number of people with diabetes has been steadily increasing in recent years. Furthermore, the statistics provided by the American Diabetes Association show that about thirty-four million Americans, or 10.5 percent of the American population, has diabetes. This is even more concerning when we consider that a significant number of people are not aware that they have diabetes, or a condition called *prediabetes* where blood sugar levels are higher than normal but not yet in the range that would qualify for a medical diagnosis of diabetes. It is important to prevent diabetes when possible and to detect it as early as possible because it can lead to a wide range of health problems, including heart disease, stroke, kidney disease, blindness, and nerve damage.

Preventing and managing diabetes requires addressing both medical and social issues. The root causes of disease and health are often social and include lack of access to healthy food options, poverty, lack of health insurance, and limited opportunities for healthy lifestyles. The medical management of diabetes requires ongoing monitoring of blood sugar levels, medication management, and lifestyle changes such as routine healthy eating and regular physical activity.

This cookbook by Jennifer Shun is transformative. She shares recipes that will help keep blood sugar levels within recommended ranges, without compromising flavor. This book can be an important tool in creating and maintaining a healthy delicious diet. Healthy diets are particularly important for people with diabetes because foods can have a significant impact on blood sugar levels. When someone has diabetes, their body either cannot produce enough insulin or cannot use insulin effectively, which can result in high levels of glucose (sugar) in the bloodstream.

Carefully choosing the right foods and following a healthy eating plan can help manage blood sugar levels and prevent complications associated with diabetes. Healthy diets for people with diabetes should include vegetables, fruits, whole grains, lean proteins, and nuts and seeds; all the while delivering a nutrient profile of healthy fats, protein, complex carbohydrates, fiber, micronutrients, and minerals.

Overall, a healthy diet is an essential part of managing diabetes and can help prevent complications associated with the condition. It's important to work with a healthcare professional or a registered dietitian to develop a personalized eating plan that fits your individual needs and preferences. The primary goals for nutrition management will be to: a) help control blood sugar levels by identifying a balanced diet that can be eaten to help keep blood sugar levels stable; b) maintain a healthy body weight because being overweight can worsen insulin resistance and increase the risk of complications associated with diabetes; c) prevent complications such as heart disease, stroke, and kidney disease; and d) provide energy to manage your diabetes and stay active.

In *For Good Measure*, Jennifer Shun provides a variety of healthy recipes for breakfast, salads, soups, sides, main meals, and snacks. The recipes prioritize healthy eating, offering options that are not only delicious, but can work with busy schedules. This cookbook allows you to explore new cuisines and flavors, while learning some new techniques for cooking and preparing food. It gives step-by-step instructions as well as information on ingredients, measurements, cooking times, techniques, and nutritional details. Appealing to both novice and expert cooks alike, you are likely to find inspiration for healthy meals and new ways to use ingredients, allowing you to plan your everyday menu or something for a special occasion.

Jennifer Shun's work makes an important contribution to promoting health for patients with diabetes or for those wanting to prevent diabetes, reduce the risk of heart disease, improve overall health, and live longer, healthier lives.

Introduction

We live a bit differently on the West Coast, as light guides the rhythm of our days. It's ever-present, beginning as a slice of cotton-candy pink peeking over the eastern hills. Soon replaced by mid-day's harsh glare, a time when the ocean sparkles, green plants work themselves into a photosynthesis frenzy, and honeybees dart among the wild sage. Shadows eventually elongate into an array of color spanning the horizon as the sun slowly sinks under the ebb and flow of the tide. A quiet arrives, signaling us to gather, reflect, and cherish the comforts of home.

Comfort means different things to different people. For me, it has always been tied to food and its ability to nurture both body and soul. My best memories are around the dinner table. Twinkling candlelight highlighting plates smeared with the remains of a meal well-enjoyed. It is from this place that I feel most connected to life—my home, the seasons, family both near and far, and the cycle of generations we honor and nourish so we all may thrive and prosper. It's wholly comforting to care for those you love with your heart and hands, and I consider it one of life's greatest joys.

In May 2016, my eldest daughter lost an enormous amount of weight despite an insatiable appetite; and I found her drinking copious amounts of water from questionable sources including the bidet. She complained of blurry vision, a constant stomachache, and her body smelled oddly fruity.

On Mother's Day, she was diagnosed with Type 1 diabetes. We took up residence at the hospital, met with an army of doctors, and enrolled in a high-speed crash course on how to be a pancreas. A week later, we staggered home armed with insulin pens, blood testers, textbooks, and an insulin-to-carbohydrate scale. In a haze of fear and anxiety, I held Mia's fragile hand and reassured her that everything would be fine. Later that evening, attempting to make dinner, I collapsed in my kitchen and sobbed. Not for the innumerable tasks and challenges that lay ahead, but for the freedom lost.

Every mountain has a footpath to the summit and the book you are holding represents our Type 1 diabetes ascent. After that initial night, I read, researched, and began stirring. Mia tasted, friends and family sampled, and my kitchen buzzed. We lit candles once more and celebrated, because if we had learned nothing else—life itself is a celebration.

There is something very real about cooking at home. It's a commitment you make to yourself and the people around you. It nurtures your sense of well-being because what we eat affects how we feel, and in no greater example than a person living with diabetes.

Like many, I believe staying connected to our food not only benefits our personal health, but also the welfare of our planet. Eating seasonally ensures meals are flavored from fresh, ripe produce, providing not only better taste, but essential vitamins and nutrients. At the same time, home cooking allows us the opportunity to shop locally at markets and farmstands that support our communities and decrease environmental waste. For me, California influences not only my soul, but my kitchen and what inevitably lands on my table. It is my hope as you navigate this book, you will find inspiration for yours.

How to Use This Book

When diabetes entered my kitchen, I struggled and failed to make my favorite recipes work for my daughter's carb-conscious diet. She was on a blood sugar roller-coaster and couldn't seem to get off.

Over the initial months, we discovered through trial and error that a low-carbohydrate menu made blood sugar management easier. I finally had a starting point—but then the real work began. I pored through recipes and revised, tested and tasted, edited out the bland, and laboriously carb-counted each one.

Whether you have prediabetes and are looking to incorporate diabetic-friendly recipes into your arsenal or are newly diagnosed and researching your next step, let's start at the beginning, so we're both on the same page as you explore this book.

LOW CARBOHYDRATE

While documenting diabetes dates to the ancient Egyptians, insulin therapy is only a century old. Before modern medicine, carbohydrate restriction was the favored treatment. Although it goes without saying, in the absence of insulin, the mortality rate was exceedingly high. However, the basic premise that blood sugar rises and falls more gently after eating a meal low in carbohydrates has been understood for thousands of years.

To explain this further, let's begin with the baseline that carbohydrates convert to glucose, which the human body uses for energy. Simply stated, our cells are hungry, and glucose is their favorite meal.

Carbohydrates fall into several categories: sugar, starch, and fiber. Sugar can be naturally occurring such as in fruit, or processed as in cane sugar. Starch includes root vegetables, beans, legumes, and whole grains, while fiber is simply the indigestible component of plant-based foods.

Carbohydrates are present in most of the foods we eat—the toast you had with breakfast, the apple-a-day snack you thought the doctor ordered, and even that cauliflower crust pizza you thought had none.

So how does this affect blood sugar? Let's circle back to the time-tested low carbohydrate diet. The fewer carbohydrates in a food, the less glucose in the blood stream and ultimately the more stable your blood sugar.

So how do we determine how many carbohydrates are in a recipe? The answer is in the nutritional data.

First understand, a total carbohydrate value represents all sugar, starch, and fiber in a given food. However, as fiber is indigestible and therefore does not affect blood sugar like sugar and starch, it can be subtracted from the total carbohydrate number to provide an adjusted value known as net carbs.

The recipes in this book incorporate this premise. They contain high fiber and no processed sugar, and therefore have a low net carb value. Additionally, they focus on natural ingredients sourced from plants and animals with minimal processing, embodying what I like to think of as the trifecta of a food-based way to prevent and manage diabetes. Lean proteins, low carbohydrates, and healthy fats and oils.

THE TRIFECTA

Let's begin with the superstar—protein. Protein provides energy without being converted to glucose and helps stabilize blood sugar by slowing down the digestion of carbohydrates.

The recipes in this book feature lean, nutrient-rich protein sources to keep your appetite satisfied. Eggs, dairy, poultry, fish, beans, legumes, pulses, nuts, and seeds all debut in delicious combinations.

As I mentioned, carbohydrates convert to glucose, which our bodies use as energy. Therefore, as they directly affect blood glucose levels, I am selective in how I incorporate carbohydrates into my recipes. High-fiber favorites in the form of nutrient-dense, non-starchy vegetables are frequently used, giving us the bonus of working more produce into our diet. Fruit, dark chocolate, maple syrup, and honey are highlighted and only at times when absolutely needed or as a special treat.

Sauces and condiments add flavor, elevating something simple to simply unexpected. I rely on healthy dressings, dips, and spreads to create depth and flavor, eliminating the need for excess salt and sweeteners.

NUTRITIONAL DATA

Every one of us approaches diabetes from a different backstory. In my kitchen, these recipes are on my table, served as leftovers, and in continual rotation. However, you may be looking for a once-weekly meal to balance your diet, perhaps a pick-me-up for a friend living with diabetes, or maybe a home-cooked dish you don't want to develop or carb count. For that reason, each recipe contains a brief nutritional overview including serving size, yield, calories, net carbs, total carbs, fat, protein, and fiber.

For ease of use, I rely both on my kitchen scale as well as standard measuring cups and spoons. Not only are these tools accessible in most home kitchens, but I also find using them to be helpful to visually understand portion size. Ask anyone what one-quarter cup of peanuts looks like and you'll quickly understand. Sometimes you simply don't have an ingredient and the grocery store is closed. Note that substitutions will negate the provided nutritional information.

WELL-BEING

We all know modern life is busy. Pre-packaged, processed foods with clear, concise nutrition labels are tempting to turn to, especially as you navigate the beginning of this disease. However, vibrant, nutrient-dense meals crafted from fresh, ethically sourced ingredients are essential for health and well-being. It is from this place, that I share this book with you. So, take a deep breath, tie on an apron, and create something nourishing. I'm hoping with both my heart and hands it will make your life a little more flavorful.

Cooking Basics

Weeknights can be hectic: some nights call for celebration and other nights snacks replace meals. My hope is you'll find something that resonates wherever you are when you open this book.

For me, kitchen success lies solely in being organized. I meal plan for the week ahead and shop accordingly. Perhaps that's more time than you're willing to commit to, but I do recommend testing and identifying dishes you enjoy and incorporating them into your rotation. Repeated practice hones your skills, and often-used ingredients become pantry staples.

The recipes in this book include the following ingredients and tools. I've strived for short ingredient lists and concise instructions, as I know we have varying skill levels in the kitchen. Growing up in the Midwest, I'm aware there can be seasonal limitations, depending upon where we live, and have aimed to utilize commonly stocked fruits and vegetables. However, some recipes feature items that may be difficult to source locally; I have found these items are available online.

STAPLE INGREDIENTS

Beans, Legumes & Pulses

While high in carbohydrates, these are also high in protein, fiber, vitamins and minerals. I have focused on lower net carb options including cannellini beans, garbanzo beans, peanuts, and soybeans to accent a recipe, rather than serve as its focus.

Cacao

Made from fermented, dried, and roasted seeds of the cacao tree, cacao finds its way into our ingredient lists in two forms: powdered and as 85% dark chocolate. While both originate from the same source and boast similar health benefits, their processing lends a different end-product. I recommend using the highest quality you can afford, understanding every manufacturer's product has a unique flavor.

Cheese

High in fat, low in carbs, and delicious as well. It's always great to have a few varieties on hand, including soft varieties like Brie, feta, goat, and ricotta; semi-soft ones such as mozzarella and blue; semi-firm cheddar; and hard Parmesan.

Fats & Oils

Healthy fats are essential to a healthy diet, as well as to impart unique flavor to recipes. Oils high in monounsaturated fats, including olive and sesame, are excellent bases for dressings. They are also stable when heated, so I use them often in cooking. Grapeseed oil is virtually flavorless with a high smoke point, so it works well as a neutral base. Unsalted butter lends a specific flavor and texture to recipes such as baked goods. On occasion salted is required and is noted in the ingredient list.

Flours & Meals

Grain-based flours and meals have been replaced in my recipes with alternatives including almond, chestnut, coconut, cornmeal, flax, and pecan. Grocery stores have a wonderful selection, and what is not available in-store can be sourced online.

Fruit

Raw fruit, aside from containing important vitamins, minerals, and plant compounds, also contains fiber. However, fruit truly is nature's candy, so while apples, avocados, blackberries, blueberries, lemons, limes, oranges, pears, raspberries, strawberries, and tomatoes are included in this book, they are used sparingly.

Herbs

Fresh and dried herbs are sourced from leafy plants with aromatic properties. Basil, bay leaves, chives, cilantro, lemongrass, mint, oregano, parsley, rosemary, and thyme add flavor and color, while brightening many of the recipes in this book. Dried herbs impart a deeper flavor than their fresh counterparts, so they are called out separately in the ingredient list.

Nuts & Seeds

Comprising everything from flours and crunchy accents to granolas, crackers and snacks, nuts and seeds bring a powerhouse of nutrients, antioxidants, and texture to recipes. Almonds, cashews, chia seeds, flaxseeds, hazelnuts, hemp seeds, nigella seeds, pecans, pistachios, pepitas, sesame seeds, sunflower seeds, and walnuts are featured frequently.

Soy Products

Simply categorized as unfermented, including tofu and soy milk, and fermented, including miso, tamari and tempeh, these items offer a nutrient-dense, low-carb protein originating from soybeans. Fermented soy products have been cultured with bacteria, yeast or mold and are considered easier to digest.

Spices & Seasonings

Ranging from aromatic to bitter, spices are sourced from dried roots (garlic powder, ginger, granulated onion, turmeric); seeds (anise, caraway, cardamom, coriander, cumin, fennel, gochugaru, nutmeg, paprika, red chili flakes, star anise); bark (cinnamon); flowers (cloves, saffron); and fruits and berries (allspice, black pepper, cayenne, peppercorn, sumac).

Seasonings (such as curry powder, salt, Tajin, za'atar) on the other hand, are a blend of spices, salts, sugars, and herbs created to enhance flavor. Seasonings have variety depending on their source. I use salt in three variations—table salt for cooking, fine sea salt for flavoring, and coarse sea salt for finishing. While this list is lengthy, spices and seasonings store incredibly well and what is not available locally can be easily sourced online.

Sweeteners

No amount of processed sugar or sugar substitute is considered healthy. Natural sweeteners, while having a few more nutrients than refined sugar or corn syrup, are still not ideal for blood sugar management. That said, in the few instances where a recipe requires a sweet back note, it is here that a minimal quantity of a natural sugar including apple juice, dates, honey or maple syrup is used.

Vegetables

Outside of lean protein, vegetables are the most common ingredient in my recipes. Sourcing the highest-quality, in-season produce available is key to the success of your dish. Nutrient-dense and packed with texture and flavor, vegetables fall into two major categories—above ground and below. It is a general rule that if a vegetable grows above ground it has a lower carb load.

Above ground vegetables include edible leaves (brussels sprouts, cabbage, chard, lettuce, kale, spinach); flowers (broccoli, cauliflower, Romanesco, zucchini blossoms); seeds (green beans, okra); stalks (asparagus, celery, leeks); fungi (mushrooms); and fruit (cucumber, eggplant, peppers, squash, zucchini).

Root vegetables grow underground at the base of a plant and include bulbs (fennel, garlic, green onion, onion, shallot); roots (beet, carrot, celeriac, ginger, jicama, radish, turnip); and tubers (sweet potato). They absorb water and nutrients to feed a plant. So, while they are nutritional powerhouses, low in calories, and high in antioxidants, they can also carry a heavy carb load.

Vinegars

Acid brightens the flavor of food and adds balance. From salads and sides to mains, I find myself depending on its zing to transform a simple dish into something unexpected. Apple cider, balsamic, Champagne, red wine, and rice vinegar are frequent players. I feel this is one of the pantry staples where the highest-quality option you can source goes a long way.

OTHER PANTRY ITEMS

Coconut Milk Powder is coconut meat that has been grated, pressed into milk, and heat dried. A substitute for coconut milk or coconut cream, coconut milk powder imparts the sweet flavor of fresh coconut, while acting as a thickening agent.

Garlic Paste is puréed garlic cloves blended with olive oil. It adds intense flavor and aroma and can be found in the produce section of most grocery stores.

Freeze-Dried Raspberry Powder contains raspberries that have been dehydrated through intense cold to retain their nutritional properties, then ground into a fine texture. If sourcing the powder is a challenge, pulse freeze-dried raspberries in a processor to achieve the desired consistency.

Hoisin Sauce is a sweet and spicy sauce made from miso, garlic, ginger, and spices. Commonly used in Chinese cuisine, this sauce works as a quick-reach condiment as well as a marinade.

Kombu is edible dried kelp found in most grocery stores. It imparts a delicious umami flavor and can help with digestion.

Maple Extract is a food flavoring that can be used as a substitute for pure maple syrup. It differs from maple flavoring, which derives its taste from fenugreek, rather than maple sap.

Mirin is a sweet rice wine. Similar to sake, but sweeter and with less alcohol, it adds umami and tang. If you can't find it at your local grocery store, it's available online.

Olives pack a healthy dose of antioxidants and vitamins, as well as a lot of opinion. Mild, fleshy Castelvetrano olives are a middle ground, especially if you find Kalamata too briny or textured.

Protein Powders are a matter of preference as the options are endless—organic, soy, vegan, and whey are just a few choices. The one fact to consider is the carbohydrate load of the variety you select.

Psyllium Husk is a fiber that when finely ground acts as a flour substitute, as well as creates elasticity and texture in quick breads. It is widely available in most grocery stores or online.

Sake is a Japanese alcoholic beverage made from fermented rice. For cooking purposes, source an inexpensive option or substitute with dry sherry.

Sun-Dried Tomato Paste brings a bold, concentrated flavor to soups, spreads, and sauces. Unlike traditional tomato paste, this version is made from sun-ripened tomatoes, which lends a deeper color and more intense flavor.

Tabasco Red Pepper Sauce is a classic Louisiana condiment made from red peppers, salt, and vinegar. While new varieties have been developed, I am referring to the original red sauce.

Tahini is seed butter made from ground toasted sesame seeds. A staple Middle Eastern condiment, it blends creaminess with an earthy, savory flavor.

Xanthan Gum works as a thickening agent, emulsifier, and binder in the absence of gluten. It gives nut flour breads and muffins their elasticity and shape.

MEASUREMENT NOTES

Measurement is a key factor in using this book. From portion sizes to ingredients, measurement is the tool we use to manage blood sugar.

- All ingredients utilize standard American measuring cups and spoons. I've added a metric conversion for anyone who feels more comfortable with a kitchen scale.

- All ingredients should be measured as they are specified in the ingredient list.

- Dry ingredients including flours, powders, and spices should be filled and then leveled off with a metal spatula or knife.

- Vegetables and fruits should fill the measurement cup or spoon specified, understanding their unique shapes and textures will extend slightly over the edge, as well as leave gaps in the measuring container.

- Liquid ingredients should be measured in a liquid measuring cup, ensuring that when at eye level the measurement is accurate.

TOOLS

Tools have made our lives easier. While some may love every new invention, I rely on a few time-tested workhorses to get the job done. Options abound for every budget, and I leave it to you to find the one that works best in your kitchen.

Baking Pans

The pans you have for a lifetime and dig out of the cupboard when needed are the champions of the kitchen. The rimmed baking sheet is the star player of this category, while a rimless version, muffin tin, bread pan, eight-inch square baking pan, pie dish, casserole dish, and springform pan all debut at least once in this book.

Convection Oven

Using a fan to circulate air, a convection oven creates an evenly heated environment. This is by no means a requirement for your kitchen, but if you are using a conventional model you may need to adjust cooking times.

Immersion Blender

An immersion blender makes quick work of puréeing hot soups and emulsifying dressings.

Kitchen Scale

A good kitchen scale is consistency's secret weapon. I prefer a portable, digital option, but in all honesty, the choices are endless and depend mostly on your preferences.

Measuring Cups

These are single-handedly your most basic kitchen requirement. American dry and liquid varieties, as well as graduated measuring spoons ranging from ⅛ teaspoon to one tablespoon are used in these recipes.

Nonstick Skillet

A small eight-inch skillet works great for small tasks, while a twelve-inch is large enough for all recipes without having to split your cooking time in batches. There can be a durability issue with nonstick skillets; therefore, I highly recommend using silicone utensils to best preserve their fragile coating.

Parchment

Food-safe, coated paper that is heat-resistant, non-stick and available in precut sheets or on a roll. It adds an insulating layer protecting both the food and the pan, while simplifying clean-up.

Processor

I use the term interchangeably with a small capacity food chopper. This kitchen staple chops and grinds in seconds, saving laborious kitchen prep time. I find myself grabbing my five-cup mini for most recipes, with the understanding that a larger capacity processor would complete the same task.

Saucepans & Stockpots

Three simple lidded pans have so many uses: a small 2-quart saucepan, large 4-quart saucepan, and 6-quart or larger stockpot. I specify the use of a stockpot; however an enamel-finished Dutch oven is a welcome substitution.

Slow Cooker

Nothing compares to this appliance's low, moist heat for enhancing flavor. With a little planning, it will become your best friend for hands-off, one-pot meals. If you're not looking to add on to your kitchen arsenal, use an enamel-finished Dutch oven in a 325 degree oven for one-fourth of the designated cook time.

Utensils

Aside from the standard place setting of knife, fork and spoon, a quality chef's knife for chopping, a paring knife for peeling, whisk for emulsifying, pastry brush for applying liquids, fine-mesh strainer for straining, turner for flipping, and spatula for scraping and sautéing are recommended. Invest in a quality chef's knife and silicone turners and spatulas to preserve your cookware.

Breakfast

Early morning is my favorite time. The birds chirp, then chorus, as color slowly fills the sky over the eastern hills. Marine layer blankets the coast and we wait for the crisp air to warm.

California lives and breathes by the sun. It nourishes and energizes, much like the foods we break our fast with each morning. A healthy breakfast sets the tone for the day, satisfies hunger, and helps steady blood sugar. Active mornings require a hearty meal to refuel, weekdays often demand a grab and go snack, while a lazy weekend offers time to experiment.

Some of my favorite recipes are housed in this section, because much like the time of day, breakfast is also my favored meal.

Yield: 2 | Serving Size: 1 cup
Calories: 64 Net Carbs: 7g Total Carbs: 10g Fat: 3g Protein: 1g Fiber: 3g

Detox Green Smoothie

I can't think of a better start to the day—bright, citrusy, slightly creamy with a kick of ginger. This drink slowly wakens the palate with an energizing dose of antioxidant-rich greens and hydrating cucumber.

Please note you will need a food processor or blender for this recipe.

- 1 cup (120 g) cucumber, sliced

- 1 cup (25 g) spinach

- ½ cup (65 g) Granny Smith apples, cubed

- ½ cup (118 ml) cold water

- ¼ cup (50 g) avocado, sliced

- 2 tablespoons lemon juice

- 1 tablespoon ginger root, minced

Using a processor or blender, add cucumber, spinach, apple, water, avocado, lemon juice and ginger, puréeing on high, until smooth and creamy.

Serve immediately over ice.

Yield: 4 | Serving Size: 1 cup
Calories: 148   Net Carbs: 12g   Total Carbs: 12g   Fat: 8g   Protein: 8g   Fiber: 0g

Masala Chai

Fragrant, warming, nourishing—Masala Chai is milk tea simmered with spices. A beverage best sipped and savored, providing an aromatic alternative to your morning coffee. Every recipe differs slightly; mine is heavy on cardamon and ginger for both intense flavor and anti-inflammatory benefits.

- **32 green cardamom pods**

- **16 whole cloves**

- **16 whole peppercorns**

- **4 cups (946 ml) whole milk**

- **8 teaspoons loose leaf Assam tea**

- **4 inches of whole ginger root**

- **2 cinnamon sticks**

- **8 star anise pods, halved**

Using either a mortar & pestle or kitchen knife, crush or rough chop cardamom, cloves and peppercorns.

Over medium heat, warm a large saucepan.

Add crushed spices, stirring continually for two minutes, until toasted.

Add milk, tea, ginger, cinnamon and star anise.

Decrease heat to low and cover, simmering for 15 minutes, do not boil.

Remove from heat, strain and serve immediately.

Yield: 6 | Serving Size: 1 muffin
Calories: 73   Net Carbs: 5g   Total Carbs: 7g   Fat: 4g   Protein: 0g   Fiber: 2g

Blueberry Muffins

These savory rather than sweet blueberry muffins hold their own against a cup of coffee. With a dense, cornbread-like texture and slightly citrus back note, these muffins are dotted with plump, juicy blueberries. Best enjoyed straight from the oven, smeared with warm butter.

Please note you will need a food processor for this recipe.

- **3 eggs**

- **¼ cup (28 g) coconut flour**

- **2 tablespoons butter, room temperature**

- **1 tablespoon apple cider vinegar**

- **1 tablespoon maple syrup**

- **1 teaspoon orange zest, finely grated**

- **1 teaspoon vanilla**

- **¼ teaspoon baking soda**

- **½ cup (70 g) blueberries**

Preheat oven to 400°F.

Line a 6-cup muffin tin with baking cups, greasing each.

Using a processor, add eggs, flour, butter, vinegar, syrup, orange zest, vanilla and baking soda, pulsing, until well-combined.

Measure 2 tablespoons of batter into each prepared liner.

Divide blueberries into six equal parts.

Push each part into a cup of batter, repeating, until all six cups have blueberries.

Bake for 20 minutes, until golden.

Yield: 6 | **Serving Size: 1 pancake**

Calories: 240   Net Carbs: 2g   Total Carbs: 4g   Fat: 24g   Protein: 6g   Fiber: 2g

Pecan Pancakes

Nutrient-rich pecan flour makes an excellent base for this healthy twist on a breakfast classic. Crispy, nutty, naturally sweet pancakes topped with warm butter or for a more decadent treat— whipped cream. Fresh raspberries add a nice pop if you're looking for a little extra sweetness.

Please note you will need a food processor for this recipe.

- **3 eggs**
- **½ cup (110 g) cream cheese**
- **1 teaspoon maple extract**
- **⅛ teaspoon salt**
- **1 cup (85 g) pecan flour**
- **1 tablespoon butter, divided**

Preheat oven to 200°F.

Using a processor, add eggs, cream cheese, maple extract and salt, pulsing, until smooth.

Add pecan flour, pulsing, until well-combined.

Over medium heat, warm a nonstick skillet.

Melt ½ tablespoon butter in heated pan.

Pour 4 tablespoons of prepared batter onto pan, leaving space to spread.

Repeat until you have three pancakes.

Once bubbles form on the surface and the bottoms brown, flip pancakes.

Cook for 2 minutes, until brown.

Serve or store in preheated oven.

Repeat with remaining batter.

Seedy Toast *with* Apple Butter

Still-warm toast slathered with apple butter may be our favorite go-to breakfast. Slightly crunchy, with a delicious nutty taste, it pairs perfectly with creamy, naturally sweet apple butter. Seedy bread holds up to a knife straight from the oven and stores exceptionally well refrigerated for up to five days.

- 2 cups (200 g) flaxseed meal
- ¼ cup (40 g) unsalted almonds, chopped
- ¼ cup (40 g) flaxseeds
- ¼ cup (35 g) unsalted pumpkin seeds
- ¼ cup (23 g) psyllium husk
- ¼ cup (35 g) unsalted sunflower seeds
- ¼ cup (28 g) walnuts, chopped
- 2 tablespoons chia seeds
- 1 tablespoon baking powder
- ¼ teaspoon salt
- ¼ cup (57 g) butter, melted
- 5 egg whites
- 2 eggs
- ½ cup (118 ml) buttermilk
- ¾ cup (210 g) apple butter

Preheat oven to 350°F.

Line a bread pan with parchment.

In a large bowl, add flaxseed meal, almonds, flaxseeds, pumpkin seeds, psyllium husk, sunflower seeds, walnuts, chia seeds, baking powder and salt, stirring, until well-combined.

In a small bowl, add melted butter, egg whites, eggs and buttermilk, whisking, until well-combined.

Add egg mixture to flax mixture, stirring, until well-combined.

Transfer batter to prepared bread pan.

Bake for 40 minutes, until golden.

Remove from pan to cool.

Once room temperature, slice into twelve equal pieces.

Toast until golden.

Serve each toasted slice with one tablespoon apple butter.

Apple Butter

Please note you will need a slow cooker and an immersion blender for this recipe.

- **Nonstick cooking spray**

- **9 cups (1.17 kg) Gala apples, cored & sliced**

- **½ cup (118 ml) water**

- **1 teaspoon cinnamon**

- **½ teaspoon ginger**

- **¼ teaspoon cloves**

Coat the slow cooker crock with nonstick cooking spray.

Add apples, water, cinnamon, ginger and cloves, stirring, until mixed.

Cover and cook on low for 9 hours.

Using an immersion blender, purée cooked apple mixture, until smooth.

Remove lid and cook for an additional 30 minutes, or until desired consistency.

Store refrigerated in a sealed, glass container.

Yield: 12 | Serving Size: 1 slice + 1 tablespoon apple butter

Calories: 313   Net Carbs: 6g   Total Carbs: 19g   Fat: 23g   Protein: 10g   Fiber: 13g

Cornbread Muffins *with* Maple Butter

Inspired by the Southern-style classic, these cornbread muffins are savory, unsweetened, and crumbly. High-quality, fresh cornmeal is the key ingredient, while maple butter adds just a tinge of sweetness, rounding out the flavors. The perfect accompaniment to your morning eggs and bacon.

Please note you will need an electric mixer for this recipe.

- ¼ cup (30 g) almond flour
- ¼ cup (35 g) fine grind cornmeal
- 1 teaspoon baking powder
- ¼ teaspoon salt
- 2 eggs
- ¼ cup (57 g) butter, room temperature
- ¼ cup (65 g) unsweetened plain yogurt
- ¼ cup (77 g) maple butter

Preheat oven to 350°F.

Line an 8-cup muffin pan with liners.

In a small bowl, add almond flour, cornmeal, baking powder and salt, stirring, until combined.

Set aside.

Separate eggs, reserving egg whites.

Using an electric mixer, cream egg yolks and butter.

Add yogurt and flour mixture, mixing, until well-combined.

Transfer batter to a clean bowl, set aside.

Wash and dry beaters.

Using an electric mixer, whip egg whites on low, until frothy.

Increase speed to high, whipping, until soft peaks form.

Fold whipped egg whites into batter.

Measure 2 tablespoons of batter into each lined muffin cup.

Bake for 15 minutes, until golden.

Serve each with ½ tablespoon maple butter.

Maple Butter

Please note you will need an electric mixer for this recipe.

- ¼ cup (57 g) unsalted butter, room temperature

- 1 tablespoon maple syrup

- ⅛ teaspoon cinnamon

- ⅛ teaspoon sea salt

Using an electric mixer, beat butter, until light and fluffy.

Add maple syrup, cinnamon and sea salt, mixing, until well-combined.

Store refrigerated in a sealed, glass container.

Yield: 8 | Serving Size: 1 muffin + ½ tablespoon maple butter

Calories: 168   Net Carbs: 5g   Total Carbs: 7g   Fat: 15g   Protein: 4g   Fiber: 2g

Yield: 12 | Serving Size: ½ cup
Calories: 389   Net Carbs: 8g   Total Carbs: 15g   Fat: 33g   Protein: 13g   Fiber: 7g

Peanut Butter Granola

Everyone needs a go-to granola recipe in their arsenal. Sweet, crunchy peanuts shine against a background of nuts and seeds. The texture is layered with a toasty, nutty flavor followed by a slightly sweet back note. This granola is perfect with milk or by the handful straight out of the jar.

- 1½ cups (240 g) unsalted almonds

- 1½ cups (210 g) unsalted peanuts

- 1 cup (80 g) unsweetened shredded coconut

- ¼ cup (40 g) flaxseeds

- ¼ cup (30 g) vanilla protein powder

- ½ cup (140 g) peanut butter

- ¼ cup (57 g) butter

- 2 tablespoons water

- 1 tablespoon honey

- 2 teaspoons vanilla

Preheat oven to 325°F.

Line a rimmed baking sheet with parchment.

Using a chef's knife, rough chop almonds and peanuts.

In a large bowl, add almonds, peanuts, coconut, flaxseeds and protein powder, stirring, until combined.

Set aside.

Over medium heat, warm a small saucepan.

Add peanut butter and butter, stirring often, until melted and combined.

Remove from heat.

Add water, honey and vanilla to peanut butter mixture, stirring, until well-combined.

Pour melted peanut butter mixture over dry ingredients, mixing, until well-combined.

Spread evenly on prepared baking sheet.

Bake for 20 minutes, until golden brown with crispy edges.

Cool before storing in a sealed, glass container.

Yogurt Cups *with* Spiced Granola & Berries

Speculaas spice cookies are the inspiration behind this crunchy and aromatic granola. Layered against tangy yogurt and sweet strawberries, these yogurt cups are an explosion of flavor. While some recipes meld better with time, this version is best served immediately.

- **4 cups (568 g) strawberries, sliced**
- **4 cups (1.04 kg) unsweetened plain yogurt**
- **2⅔ cups (320 g) spiced granola**

In eight 12-ounces glasses, add ½ cup (70 g) strawberries to each.

Follow with ½ cup (130 g) yogurt.

Finish with ⅓ cup (40 g) granola.

Serve immediately.

Yield: 8 | Serving Size: 1 yogurt cup

Calories: 351   Net Carbs: 13g   Total Carbs: 21g   Fat: 27g   Protein: 11g   Fiber: 8g

Spiced Granola

- ½ cup (80 g) unsalted almonds

- ½ cup (40 g) unsweetened shredded coconut

- ½ cup (80 g) flaxseeds

- ¼ cup (40 g) sesame seeds

- ¼ cup (35 g) raw pumpkin seeds

- 2 tablespoons chia seeds

- 2 teaspoons flaxseed meal

- 1 teaspoon cinnamon

- ⅛ teaspoon ground anise seed

- ⅛ teaspoon cardamom

- ⅛ teaspoon cloves

- ⅛ teaspoon ginger

- ⅛ teaspoon nutmeg

- ⅛ teaspoon white pepper

- ⅛ teaspoon salt

- ¼ cup (57 g) unsalted butter

- 1 teaspoon maple syrup

- ½ teaspoon vanilla

Preheat oven to 325°F.

Line a rimmed baking sheet with parchment.

With a chef's knife, rough chop almonds.

In a large bowl, add almonds, coconut, flaxseeds, sesame seeds, pumpkin seeds, chia seeds, flaxseed meal, spices and salt, stirring, until combined.

Set aside.

In a microwave-safe bowl, heat butter in microwave for 30 seconds, until melted.

Add syrup and vanilla to melted butter, stirring, until combined.

Pour butter mixture over dry ingredients, stirring, until well-combined.

Spread evenly on prepared baking sheet.

Bake for 20 minutes, until light brown with crispy edges.

Yield: 4 | Serving Size: ½ cup

Calories: 235   Net Carbs: 4g   Total Carbs: 6g   Fat: 19g   Protein: 12g   Fiber: 2g

Tofu Scramble *with* Blistered Tomatoes

Tofu is extremely versatile. Mild, textured, and flavor absorbent, it provides an alternative protein source for those following a special diet or looking to add variety. Quick in preparation, bold in flavor, the tofu in this recipe soaks up the deep, rich, umami flavor of the tamari and contrasts beautifully against sweet, roasted cherry tomatoes.

- 1 cup (150 g) cherry tomatoes
- ¼ cup (59 ml) olive oil, divided
- ⅛ teaspoon salt
- 6 cups (150 g) spinach
- 16 ounces (450 g) firm tofu, drained & crumbled
- ¼ cup (12 g) chives, chopped
- 1 tablespoon reduced-sodium tamari
- ⅛ teaspoon black pepper

Preheat oven to 450°F.

Line a small, rimmed baking sheet with parchment.

In a small bowl, add tomatoes and one tablespoon olive oil, stirring, until well-coated.

Arrange tomatoes on prepared sheet.

Sprinkle with salt and roast for 20 minutes, until blistered.

Over medium heat, warm a nonstick skillet.

Add one tablespoon olive oil to heated pan.

Add spinach, sautéing several minutes, until wilted.

Transfer cooked spinach to a clean bowl, set aside.

Over medium heat, rewarm nonstick skillet.

Add remaining olive oil to heated pan.

Add tofu, sautéing several minutes, until heated through.

Add chives, stirring, until combined.

Add cooked spinach, tamari and pepper, stirring, until combined.

Remove from heat and top with blistered tomatoes.

Yield: 12 | Serving Size: 2
Calories: 101 Net Carbs: 1g Total Carbs: 2g Fat: 8g Protein: 6g Fiber: 1g

Deviled Eggs

Chilled halos of egg salad with a spicy red pepper kick. Deviled eggs have fallen in and out of favor since Medieval times. More layered than a simple hard boiled egg and perfect for a quick, yet savory, protein boost when time is limited, this classic is making a comeback.

- **12 large eggs**

- **8 cups (1.9 L) cold water**

- **¼ cup (30 g) celery, finely chopped**

- **¼ cup (60 g) mayonnaise**

- **¼ cup (65 g) pickle relish, drained**

- **3 tablespoons chives, finely chopped**

- **1 tablespoon yellow mustard**

- **2 teaspoons parsley, finely chopped**

- **¼ teaspoon salt**

- **⅛ teaspoon black pepper**

- **⅛ teaspoon Tabasco red pepper sauce**

- **½ teaspoon coarse sea salt**

Place eggs in a single layer in the bottom of a large saucepan.

Add water and cover.

Over high heat, bring eggs to a rolling boil.

Remove from heat and let stand for 12 minutes.

Drain and resubmerge cooked eggs in cold water, until cooled.

Peel eggs and halve lengthwise.

Scoop yolks and transfer to a clean bowl, set aside both halved eggs and yolks.

In a separate small bowl, add celery, mayonnaise, pickle relish, chives, mustard, parsley, salt, pepper and red pepper sauce, stirring, until well-combined.

Add yolks to mayonnaise mixture, mashing, until combined.

Fill each egg half with one tablespoon of filling.

Sprinkle with coarse sea salt.

Serve chilled or store refrigerated.

Herbed Chickpeas & Wilted Spinach *with* Crispy Egg

This recipe pan roasts chickpeas for a nutty, buttery crunch then adds in fresh herbs for extra flavor. Served with a side of garlicky, wilted spinach and topped with a crispy, runny fried egg, it's perfect for a hearty breakfast or quick weeknight dinner.

• 3 tablespoons olive oil, divided	Over medium heat, warm a large, nonstick skillet.
• 3 teaspoons garlic, minced & divided	Add one tablespoon olive oil to heated pan.
	Add 2 teaspoons garlic, sautéing for 30 seconds, until fragrant.
• 15 ounces (425 g) garbanzo beans, drained	Add garbanzo beans, ½ teaspoon salt and pepper, stirring, until combined.
• 1 teaspoon salt, divided	
• ¼ teaspoon black pepper	Cook, stirring occasionally, until beans have crisped and split.
• ⅓ cup (10 g) basil, chopped	Remove from heat.
• ⅓ cup (16 g) chives, finely chopped	Add basil, chives, parsley, tossing, until combined.
• ⅓ cup (10 g) parsley, chopped	Transfer ¼ cup (approximately 160 g) herbed chickpeas to each of four plates, set aside.
• ¼ cup (36 g) onion, finely chopped	Over medium heat, rewarm nonstick skillet.
• ½ teaspoon ginger, minced	Add one tablespoon olive oil to heated pan.
• 4 cups (100 g) spinach	Add onion, ginger and remaining garlic, sautéing, until tender.
• 4 eggs	Add spinach and remaining salt, sautéing, until wilted.
• ¹⁄₁₆ teaspoon coarse sea salt	Remove from heat.
	Add ¼ cup (20 g) wilted spinach to each of the plated herbed chickpeas, set aside.
	Over medium heat, rewarm nonstick skillet.

Add remaining olive oil to heated pan.

Add eggs, cooking, until edges are golden brown.

Tilt skillet slightly, spooning pooled oil over egg whites, until cooked through.

Top each plate with crispy egg.

Sprinkle with coarse sea salt.

Serve immediately.

Yield: 4 | Serving Size: 1 plate

Calories: 271   Net Carbs: 13g   Total Carbs: 19g   Fat: 17g   Protein: 13g   Fiber: 6g

Yield: 8 | Serving Size: 1 slice
Calories: 162 Net Carbs: 5g Total Carbs: 6g Fat: 11g Protein: 9g Fiber: 1g

Savory Frittata

A frittata is similar to an omelet but differs in preparation. Whisking air into the eggs and cream increases volume, creating a creamy texture. Sweet potato, red pepper, cumin, and tangy feta add an unexpected pop of flavor to this slow-baked breakfast or brunch staple.

- 1 tablespoon olive oil

- 1 cup (150 g) sweet potato, peeled & chopped

- ½ cup (40 g) red pepper, chopped

- ¼ cup (12 g) green onion, chopped

- 1 teaspoon cumin

- 1 teaspoon salt, divided

- 2 cups (50 g) spinach, chopped

- 1 cup (120 g) feta, crumbled

- 8 eggs

- 2 tablespoons heavy cream

- 2 teaspoons garlic, minced

- ⅛ teaspoon black pepper

Preheat oven to 325°F.

Coat a 9-inch pie dish with cooking spray.

Over medium heat, warm a small, nonstick skillet.

Add olive oil to heated pan.

Add sweet potato, red pepper and green onion, sautéing, until golden brown.

Add cumin and ½ teaspoon salt, stirring, until combined.

Reduce heat to low and cover, cooking, until sweet potato is fork tender.

Add spinach and cover, cooking, until wilted.

Distribute vegetable mixture in a single layer in the bottom of the prepared pie dish.

Sprinkle with feta.

In a small bowl, add eggs, heavy cream, remaining salt, garlic and pepper, whisking, until well-blended.

Pour egg mixture over vegetables and cheese.

Bake for 35 minutes, until center is set.

Salads

We celebrate the change of seasons with produce. Spring arrives along with tender lettuces and crunchy peas; the intense summer sun infuses vibrant flavors and colors, while autumn's sweet and savory cornucopia contrasts sharpy against winter's crispy brassicas.

Our salad bowl showcases the season's bounty together with layers of texture, aromas, and punchy dressings. It also reflects the day—summer's hot, bright light pairs perfectly with a crunchy, vivid salad for a light, alfresco dinner, while savory, hearty greens balance a heavy protein main when the weather is chilly.

All on the backstory that nutrient-dense, fiber rich, low in carbohydrate vegetables are the central component of a healthy diet.

Yield: 8 | Serving Size: 1 ½ cups
Calories: 168   Net Carbs: 7g   Total Carbs: 11g   Fat: 12g   Protein: 7g   Fiber: 4g

Spring Salad *with* Rosemary Vinaigrette

Delicate bib lettuce is the base for this spring salad featuring tender green beans and chanterelle mushrooms. A savory rosemary vinaigrette adds an element of earthiness, while creamy, sharp cheddar rounds out the flavors. Heat from the cooked vegetables will quickly wilt the fragile lettuces, so it's best to put everything together right before you are ready to serve.

- **2 teaspoons olive oil, divided**
- **2 cups (200 g) green beans**
- **1 cup (150 g) shelled edamame**
- **6 sprigs fresh thyme**
- **1 cup (40 g) chanterelle mushrooms**
- **1 teaspoon Worcestershire sauce**
- **¼ cup (59 ml) extra-virgin olive oil**
- **2 tablespoons white balsamic vinegar**
- **1 tablespoon fresh rosemary needles, chopped**
- **½ teaspoon mayonnaise**
- **½ teaspoon sea salt**
- **8 cups (200 g) bib lettuce**
- **½ cup (65 g) white cheddar, chopped**

Over medium heat, warm a nonstick skillet.

Add one teaspoon olive oil to heated pan.

Add green beans, edamame and thyme, sautéing several minutes, until tender.

Transfer cooked beans to a large salad bowl and discard thyme sprigs.

Over medium heat, rewarm the nonstick skillet.

Add remaining olive oil to heated pan.

Add mushrooms, sautéing several minutes, until lightly browned.

Add Worcestershire sauce, stirring, until well-coated.

Add mushrooms to the large salad bowl, tossing to combine with cooked beans.

In a small bowl, add extra-virgin olive oil, vinegar, rosemary, mayonnaise and salt, whisking, until well-combined.

Add half the vinaigrette to the large salad bowl, tossing to coat cooked beans and mushrooms.

Add lettuce and remaining vinaigrette, tossing until just combined.

Top with cheddar and serve immediately.

Mixed Greens Salad *with* Citrus, Beets, Fennel & Pistachio Butter

Inspired by winter's citrus season and topped with creamy, decadent pistachio butter, lightly dressed mixed lettuces create a neutral base for juicy orange slices, earthy beets, and raw licorice-flavored fennel. The pistachio butter can be made ahead and refrigerated, but is best served room temperature.

- 2 cups (360 g) beets, quartered
- 1 tablespoon olive oil
- ⅛ teaspoon sea salt
- ⅛ cup (30 ml) extra-virgin olive oil
- 1 tablespoon Dijon mustard
- 1 tablespoon lemon juice
- 1 tablespoon Champagne vinegar
- ½ tablespoon honey
- ½ teaspoon garlic, minced
- ¼ teaspoon black pepper
- ¼ teaspoon salt
- ⅛ teaspoon Tabasco red pepper sauce
- 8 cups (200 g) mixed lettuces
- 2 cups (280 g) fennel bulb, thinly sliced
- 2 cups (350 g) orange, peeled & sliced

- ½ cup (68 g) pistachio meats, chopped
- ½ cup (160 g) pistachio butter

Preheat oven to 400°F.

Line a small, rimmed baking sheet with parchment.

In a small bowl, toss beets in olive oil.

Sprinkle with sea salt, transfer to prepared pan and roast for 40 minutes, until tender.

In a small bowl, add extra-virgin olive oil, mustard, lemon juice, vinegar, honey, garlic, pepper, salt and red pepper sauce, whisking, until well-combined.

Add half the vinaigrette and lettuces to a large salad bowl, tossing to coat.

On eight plates, add one cup (approximately 25 g) of dressed greens.

Follow with ¼ cup (45 g) roasted beets, ¼ cup (35 g) fennel and ¼ cup (44 g) orange slices.

Drizzle with remaining vinaigrette and top with one tablespoon pistachios.

Serve immediately with one tablespoon pistachio butter.

Pistachio Butter

Please note you will need a food processor for this recipe.

- **⅔ cup (90 g) pistachio meats**

- **¼ cup (59 ml) extra-virgin olive oil**

- **1 teaspoon maple syrup**

- **¼ teaspoon sea salt**

Using a processor, blend pistachio meats, extra-virgin olive oil, maple syrup and sea salt, until smooth and creamy.

Store refrigerated in a sealed, glass container.

Yield: 8 | Serving Size: 1½ cups salad + 1 tablespoon pistachio butter

Calories: 288   Net Carbs: 15g   Total Carbs: 22g   Fat: 21g   Protein: 8g   Fiber: 7g

Yield: 10 | Serving Size: 1 cup

Calories: 70   Net Carbs: 6g   Total Carbs: 8g   Fat: 4g   Protein: 1g   Fiber: 2g

Crunchy Slaw *with* Ginger Orange Vinaigrette

Picnics, barbeques, buffets—we all need a salad that stands up to time unrefrigerated. Nutty, toasted sesame oil layers against bright citrus and fresh ginger with an unexpected kick of red chili pepper. Crunchy, slightly spicy, and colorful, this slaw elevates your favorite sandwich and pairs perfectly with seafood. Crisp cabbage holds up well in the refrigerator, making it an ideal leftover.

- 8 cups (560 g) cabbage, shredded
- 1 teaspoon salt
- ¼ cup (59 ml) fresh orange juice
- 2 tablespoons toasted sesame oil
- 2 tablespoons rice vinegar
- 1 tablespoon ginger, minced
- ½ tablespoon maple syrup
- 1 teaspoon mayonnaise
- 1 teaspoon red chili flakes
- ½ teaspoon sea salt
- 2 cups (150 g) carrots, shredded
- ¼ cup (12 g) chives, minced
- ⅛ cup (20 g) toasted sesame seeds

In a large salad bowl, add cabbage and salt, tossing, until combined.

Let rest for 30 minutes.

In a small bowl, add orange juice, sesame oil, vinegar, ginger, maple syrup, mayonnaise, chili flakes and sea salt, whisking, until well-combined.

Add half the vinaigrette to cabbage, tossing to coat.

Add carrots, chives and remaining vinaigrette, tossing to combine.

Top with sesame seeds and serve.

Roasted Market Salad
with **Romesco**

Summer's eggplants, peppers, beans, and squash shine in this composed market salad. Cauliflower adds texture while spicy, slightly smoky romesco is the perfect finish. If the weather is too hot for the oven, grilling is always an option. The preparation is the same, but over medium heat, the cook time will be much shorter.

- 3 cups (405 g) cauliflower florets
- 3 cups (255 g) eggplant, cubed
- ¼ cup (59 ml) olive oil, divided
- 1 teaspoon salt, divided
- 3 cups (240 g) bell pepper, sliced
- 3 cups (300 g) green beans, trimmed
- 3 cups (450 g) zucchini, sliced
- ¾ teaspoon coarse sea salt
- 3 tablespoons parsley, minced
- 1½ cups (420 g) romesco

Preheat oven to 400°F.

Line three rimmed baking sheets with parchment.

Arrange cauliflower and eggplant on one prepared sheet.

Brush vegetables with 2 tablespoons olive oil.

Sprinkle with ½ teaspoon salt, roasting for 30 minutes, until golden brown and tender.

Arrange bell pepper on second prepared sheet.

Brush with one tablespoon olive oil.

Roast for 20 minutes, until tender.

Arrange green beans and zucchini on remaining prepared sheet.

Brush vegetables with remaining olive oil.

Sprinkle with ½ teaspoon salt, roasting for 10 minutes, until tender.

On six plates, arrange ⅓ cup (45 g) of roasted cauliflower, ⅓ cup (50 g) eggplant, ⅓ cup (40 g) bell pepper, ⅓ cup (50 g) green beans and ⅓ cup (90 g) zucchini.

Top each with ⅛ teaspoon coarse sea salt and ½ tablespoon parsley.

Serve each warm with ¼ cup (70 g) romesco.

Romesco

Please note you will need a food processor for this recipe.

- **1 cup (260 g) roasted red peppers**

- **½ cup (80 g) Marcona almonds**

- **¼ cup (8 g) parsley, chopped**

- **2 tablespoons extra-virgin olive oil**

- **2 tablespoons sun-dried tomato paste**

- **2 tablespoons red wine vinegar**

- **1 teaspoon garlic, minced**

- **1 teaspoon paprika**

- **1 teaspoon red chili flakes**

- **1 teaspoon sea salt**

~~~~~~~~~~~~~~~~~~~~~~~~~~~~~~~~~

Using a processor, blend roasted red peppers, almonds, parsley, olive oil, tomato paste, vinegar, garlic, paprika, red chili flakes and sea salt, until thick and slightly chunky.

Store refrigerated in a sealed, glass container.

Yield: 6 | Serving Size: 2½ cups salad + ¼ cup romesco

Calories: 266   Net Carbs: 12g   Total Carbs: 20g   Fat: 20g   Protein: 7g   Fiber: 8g

Yield: 6 | Serving Size: 1 cup
Calories: 278   Net Carbs: 5g   Total Carbs: 9g   Fat: 26g   Protein: 7g   Fiber: 4g

Winter Greens Salad *with* Blueberries, Pecans & Goat Cheese

Nutrient-rich and deeply flavored, chard and kale sweeten after a light frost, making them the ideal base for a hearty, winter salad. Dressed in a snappy, apple cider vinaigrette, dotted with crisp celery, plump blueberries, buttery pecans, and creamy goat cheese, this salad is even better if you skip the toss and massage-in the dressing.

Please note you will need a food processor for this recipe.

- **3 cups (75 g) chard, chopped**
- **3 cups (75 g) kale, chopped**
- **1 cup (100 g) pecans, divided**
- **¼ cup (59 ml) extra-virgin olive oil**
- **2 tablespoons apple cider vinegar**
- **1 teaspoon capers, drained**
- **1 teaspoon garlic, minced**
- **½ teaspoon Dijon mustard**
- **⅛ teaspoon black pepper**
- **⅛ teaspoon sea salt**
- **1 cup (140 g) blueberries**
- **1 cup (120 g) celery, diced**
- **½ cup (60 g) goat cheese, crumbled**
- **¼ cup (12 g) chives, minced**

In a large salad bowl, add chard and kale, tossing, until combined.

Using a processor, blend ¼ cup (25 g) pecans, extra-virgin olive oil, vinegar, capers, garlic, mustard, pepper and sea salt, until smooth.

Add half the vinaigrette to greens, tossing to coat.

Add remaining pecans and vinaigrette, blueberries, celery, goat cheese and chives, tossing to combine.

Serve immediately.

Yield: 6 | Serving Size: 3 cups
Calories: 268   Net Carbs: 13g   Total Carbs: 22g   Fat: 18g   Protein: 11g   Fiber: 9g

California Greek Salad

A traditional Greek village salad is a blend of sun-ripened tomatoes, cucumbers, green peppers, red onion and olives dressed in little more than red wine vinegar and olive oil. Topped with a briny slab of feta it outshines even the summer sun. As a Californian, I felt it was only appropriate to add in a hefty mix of farmstand lettuces and spicy radishes, and while the sun ripened those juicy cherry tomatoes, I had my oven coax out even more flavor.

- 1 cup (150 g) cherry tomatoes
- 1 teaspoon olive oil
- 2 cups (240 g) cucumber, chopped
- 1 cup (80 g) red bell pepper, chopped
- ½ cup (72 g) red onion, finely chopped
- ½ cup (80 g) pitted Kalamata olives
- ¼ cup (59 ml) extra-virgin olive oil
- 2 tablespoons red wine vinegar
- 1 teaspoon garlic, minced
- 1 teaspoon Dijon mustard
- 1 teaspoon oregano
- ½ teaspoon salt
- ¼ teaspoon black pepper
- 12 cups (300 g) mixed lettuces
- ¼ cup (40 g) radish, thinly sliced
- 2 tablespoons fresh oregano, minced
- 1 cup (120 g) feta, crumbled

Preheat oven to 400°F.

Line a small, rimmed baking sheet with parchment.

Arrange tomatoes on prepared sheet.

Brush with olive oil.

Roast for 20 minutes, until skins blister.

In a large salad bowl, add cucumber, bell pepper, onion and olives, tossing, until combined.

In a small bowl, add extra-virgin olive oil, vinegar, garlic, mustard, oregano, salt and pepper, whisking, until well-combined.

Add half the vinaigrette to the large salad bowl, tossing to coat cucumber mixture.

Add lettuces, radishes, fresh oregano and remaining vinaigrette, tossing to combine.

Top with roasted tomatoes and feta.

Serve immediately.

Yield: 8 | Serving Size: 1 cup
Calories: 60   Net Carbs: 2g   Total Carbs: 5g   Fat: 4g   Protein: 2g   Fiber: 3g

Kale Tabbouleh

Traditional tabbouleh's fresh herbs, juicy tomatoes, and zingy lemon dressing inspired this simple salad. Finely chopped, massaged kale replaces tender parsley, and crisp cucumber adds substance, while aromatic mint and spicy radishes add a pop of something unexpected. Served traditionally in the Levant as a side dish, this revised salad stands alone perfectly or alongside a slab of baked feta.

- 2 tablespoons lemon juice
- 2 tablespoons extra-virgin olive oil
- 1 tablespoon shallot, minced
- 1 teaspoon cumin
- ½ teaspoon salt
- 6 cups (150 g) kale, finely chopped
- 1 cup (120 g) cucumber, finely chopped
- 1 cup (140 g) tomato, finely chopped
- ½ cup (10 g) fresh mint, torn
- ½ cup (80 g) radish, thinly sliced

In a small bowl, add lemon juice, extra-virgin olive oil, shallot, cumin and salt, whisking, until blended.

In a large salad bowl, add kale and vinaigrette, massaging, until slightly softened.

Add cucumber, tomato, mint and radish, tossing, until just combined.

Refrigerate for 30 minutes before serving.

Yield: 6 | Serving Size: ½ cup

Calories: 170   Net Carbs: 3g   Total Carbs: 8g   Fat: 15g   Protein: 4g   Fiber: 5g

Shaved Brussels Sprouts Salad *with* Avocado

Shredding brussels sprouts may seem daunting, but your processor makes quick work of the task, breaking down the fibrous texture and mellowing any bitterness. Tossed in a bright, mustard-flavored dressing with the counterbalance of salted almonds and creamy avocado, you'll wonder why you ever shied away from this cruciferous vegetable.

- 2 cups (160 g) brussels sprouts, shredded

- 1 teaspoon salt

- 2 tablespoons lemon juice

- 2 tablespoons whole grain mustard

- 2 tablespoons extra-virgin olive oil

- 1 teaspoon garlic, minced

- ½ cup (15 g) parsley, minced

- 1 cup (200 g) avocado, sliced

- ½ cup (80 g) salted almonds, chopped

In a medium salad bowl, add brussels sprouts and salt, tossing, until combined.

Let rest for 15 minutes.

In a small bowl, add lemon juice, mustard, olive oil and garlic, whisking, until well-combined.

Add vinaigrette and parsley to brussels sprouts, tossing to coat.

Top with avocado and almonds.

Serve immediately.

Brassicas Salad *with* Hummus

This lazily composed salad pairs snappy, apple cider vinaigrette with sweet, roasted broccoli, chopped kale and shredded brussels sprouts. With contrasting silky avocado and creamy, nutty hummus, this flavorful salad is best served in season when the slightly bitter brassicas let their sweet side shine.

• 6 cups (390 g) broccoli florets	Preheat oven to 450°F.
• 2 tablespoons olive oil	Line a rimmed baking sheet with parchment.
• ½ teaspoon sea salt	Arrange broccoli on prepared sheet.
• ¼ cup (59 ml) extra-virgin olive oil	Brush with olive oil.
• ¼ cup (30 g) shallots, minced	Sprinkle with sea salt, roasting for 20 minutes, until golden brown and tender.
• 2 tablespoons apple cider vinegar	While roasting...
• 1 tablespoon Dijon mustard	In a small bowl, add extra-virgin olive oil, shallots, vinegar, mustard, garlic, pepper and salt, whisking, until well-combined.
• 1 teaspoon garlic, minced	
• ½ teaspoon black pepper	In a large salad bowl, add kale and brussels sprouts, tossing, until combined.
• ½ teaspoon salt	
• 8 cups (200 g) kale, chopped	Add half the vinaigrette to brassicas, massaging, until slightly wilted.
• 2 cups (160 g) brussels sprouts, shredded	Set aside, until removing broccoli from oven.
• ½ cup (70 g) sunflower seeds	While warm, rough chop roasted broccoli and add to wilted brassicas.
• 2 cups (400 g) avocado, sliced	Add remaining vinaigrette and sunflower seeds, tossing, until combined.
• 1½ cups (345 g) hummus	On eight plates, arrange one cup (approximately 90 g) dressed brassicas.
	Top each with ¼ cup (50 g) avocado.
	Serve warm with 3 tablespoons hummus.

Hummus

Please note you will need a food processor for this recipe.

- ¼ cup (59 ml) lemon juice

- 2 teaspoons garlic paste

- 4 cups (946 ml) warm water

- 1½ cups (240 g) cooked garbanzo beans

- ½ teaspoon baking soda

- ½ cup (128 g) tahini

- ½ teaspoon sea salt

- 2 tablespoons ice water

- 1 tablespoon extra-virgin olive oil

- ¼ teaspoon cumin

In a small bowl, combine lemon juice and garlic paste, set aside.

In a large saucepan, add water, garbanzo beans and baking soda.

Over high heat, bring beans to a boil.

Reduce heat, simmering for 20 minutes, until beans are bloated and soft.

Drain in a fine-mesh strainer.

Using a processor, blend lemon juice mixture, tahini and sea salt.

Add ice water, blending, until creamy.

Add drained garbanzo beans, extra-virgin olive oil and cumin, blending, until desired consistency.

Store refrigerated in a sealed, glass container.

Yield: 8 | Serving Size: 1 cup salad + 3 tablespoons hummus
Calories: 373   Net Carbs: 16g   Total Carbs: 27g   Fat: 28g   Protein: 11g   Fiber: 11g

Yield: 4 | Serving Size: ½ cup
Calories: 143   Net Carbs: 2g   Total Carbs: 3g   Fat: 7g   Protein: 17g   Fiber: 1g

Tuna Salad

My grandmother Joy's culinary specialty was a mean tuna salad. Given every home cook nods to those who have skilled them, this revised version is in her honor. While she would have argued for more pickles, canned tuna pairs with sweet, tart apple, chives and crunchy pepitas for a modern update to this beachside classic.

Please note you will need a food processor for this recipe.

- **12 ounces (340 g) water-packed tuna, drained**

- **½ cup (65 g) Granny Smith apple, chopped**

- **½ cup (80 g) bread & butter pickles**

- **2 tablespoons mayonnaise**

- **1 tablespoon chives, minced**

- **1 teaspoon Dijon mustard**

- **½ teaspoon sea salt**

- **¼ teaspoon black pepper**

- **1 tablespoon salted, roasted pepitas**

Using a processor, add tuna, pulsing, until finely chopped.

Transfer to a medium bowl, set aside.

Add apple and pickles to processor, pulsing, until finely chopped.

Add to tuna, mixing, until combined.

Add mayonnaise, chives, mustard, salt and pepper, mixing, until well-combined.

Top with pepitas.

Serve or store refrigerated.

Yield: 8 | Serving Size: ½ cup
Calories: 369 Net Carbs: 8g Total Carbs: 11g Fat: 28g Protein: 21g Fiber: 3g

Chicken Salad *with* Dried Cherries & Toasted Walnuts

This simple recipe can simplify further with leftover cooked chicken or a store-bought rotisserie. While toasting walnuts intensifies their aroma and crunch, you can skip this step if time is limited, as the crispy celery and tangy cherries add interest and flavor, making this a one bowl, quick-prep salad for a lunch or light weekday meal.

- 2 cups (225 g) walnuts, chopped

- 4 cups (600 g) cooked chicken, chopped

- 1 cup (120 g) celery, chopped

- ½ cup (50 g) dried cherries

- ¼ cup (36 g) red onion, finely chopped

- ⅓ cup (80 g) mayonnaise

- ¼ cup (59 ml) lemon juice

- 1 teaspoon sea salt

- ½ teaspoon black pepper

Preheat oven to 350°F.

Line a rimmed baking sheet with parchment.

Arrange walnuts in a single layer on prepared sheet.

Bake 8 minutes, tossing frequently, until golden brown.

In a medium bowl, add toasted walnuts, chicken, celery, cherries and onion, mixing, until combined.

In a small bowl, add mayonnaise, lemon juice, salt and pepper, stirring, until combined.

Add mayonnaise mixture to chicken, tossing, until well-coated.

Serve or store refrigerated.

Niçoise Salad *with* Tuna Confit

A composed, classic salad for a lazy summer evening. Time is required to work through the steps, but the velvety, poached tuna confit is worth the effort. Sun-ripened tomatoes, fresh green beans, and crisp lettuce are essential and come together quickly tossed in a light vinaigrette. Dressed potatoes have been omitted, creating an extremely low in carbohydrate, high protein meal perfect for warm weather.

- 2 pounds (908 g) fresh tuna steak
- 1 teaspoon salt
- 3 cups + 1 teaspoon (715 ml) olive oil
- 1 tablespoon thyme, minced
- 1 teaspoon peppercorns
- ½ teaspoon fennel seeds, crushed
- ½ teaspoon lemon zest
- 2 bay leaves
- 2 garlic cloves, peeled & crushed
- 8 eggs
- 8 cups (1.9 L) water
- 3 cups (300 g) green beans, trimmed
- ¼ cup (59 ml) extra-virgin olive oil
- 2 tablespoons red wine vinegar
- ½ teaspoon Dijon mustard
- ½ teaspoon sea salt

- ⅛ teaspoon black pepper
- 8 cups (200 g) bib lettuce
- 1 cup (150 g) cherry tomatoes, halved
- ¼ cup (40 g) Kalamata olives, pitted

~~~~~~~~~~~~~~~~~~~~~~~~~~~~

Trim tuna into 2-inch pieces, rub with salt and set aside.

In a large saucepan, add 3 cups (710 ml) olive oil, thyme, peppercorns, fennel seeds, lemon zest, bay leaves and garlic.

Over medium heat, bring olive oil mixture to a low simmer for 20 minutes.

Remove from heat.

Submerge salted tuna in infused olive oil.

Cover for about 5 minutes, until desired doneness.

Remove tuna from oil and set aside.

Place eggs in a single layer in the bottom of a large saucepan.

Add water and cover.

Over high heat, bring eggs to a rolling boil.

Remove from heat and let stand for 12 minutes.

Drain and run cooked eggs under cold tap water, until cooled.

Peel eggs and halve lengthwise, set aside.

Over medium heat, warm a small nonstick skillet.

Add one teaspoon olive oil to heated pan.

Add green beans, sautéing, until crisp tender.

Remove from heat.

In a small bowl, add extra-virgin olive oil, vinegar, mustard, sea salt and pepper, whisking, until well-combined.

In a large salad bowl, add lettuce, sautéed green beans, tomatoes and olives.

Add vinaigrette, tossing, until combined.

On eight plates, arrange 1½ cups (approximately 98 g) of salad mixture.

Top with 2 egg halves.

Serve with 4 ounces (113 g) of tuna confit.

Yield: 8 | Serving Size: 1½ cups salad, 1 egg + 4 ounces (113 g) tuna

Calories: 344   Net Carbs: 5g   Total Carbs: 9g   Fat: 18g   Protein: 36g   Fiber: 4g

Soups

Memories rooted in food gather all five senses, blending them into a powerful tool for cultivating well-being. For me, homemade soup may be one of my greatest triggers, seeded at a young age in my mother's kitchen. I carried this through to when my own children were young, specifically each November.

As the days grew shorter, we spent an annual beachside evening ushering in the change of light. We covered the sand with twinkling lanterns, chatted with friends against the backdrop of the crashing surf, and shared homemade soups nestled in brightly colored Dutch ovens as the sun gave its final performance of the day. It was a simple evening with profound memory because like food itself, it tickled all of our senses.

Homemade soup is nourishing as a healthy lunch or a light dinner. It honors our busy days in its ability to provide multiple, easy-to-access meals, while maintaining blood sugar when we are feeling under the weather or contemplating skipping dinner.

Yield: 8 | Serving Size: 1 cup

Calories: 90   Net Carbs: 6g   Total Carbs: 8g   Fat: 3g   Protein: 8g   Fiber: 2g

Red Miso *with* Vegetables

Deeply flavored red miso seasons this hearty vegetable soup. While bonito flakes traditionally flavor the dashi (broth) along with kombu, I omitted to create a vegan version of this classic Japanese dish. If you're looking for a little extra umami, add a splash of tamari to your bowl right before serving.

• 6 cups (1.4 L) water	In a large stockpot, combine water and kombu.
• 1 large piece of kombu	Over medium heat, simmer for 30 minutes.
• 5 garlic cloves, smashed	Discard kombu, adding garlic and ginger to broth.
• ¼ cup (30 g) ginger root, sliced	Simmer for 30 minutes.
• 2 cups (50 g) chard, chopped	Discard garlic and ginger, adding chard and carrots to broth.
• 1½ cup (240 g) carrots, sliced	Simmer for 5 minutes.
• 2 cups (340 g) firm tofu, cubed	Add tofu, zucchini and mushrooms to broth, simmering, until just tender.
• 2 cups (300 g) zucchini, sliced	
• 1 cup (90 g) beech mushrooms	Remove from heat.
• 4 tablespoons red miso paste	In a small bowl, add miso paste to ½ cup (118 ml) broth, whisking, until dissolved.
• ¼ cup (12 g) scallions, finely sliced	Add tempered miso to broth, stirring, until combined.
	Top with scallions and serve immediately.

Yield: 12 | Serving Size: 1 cup
Calories: 86 Net Carbs: 4g Total Carbs: 6g Fat: 2g Protein: 11g Fiber: 2g

Shrimp Gumbo

Traditionally served with rice, our low in carbohydrate gumbo is a little more soup than stew, with okra acting as a thickener. Shrimp broth is the base of this revised Louisiana classic. Purchasing whole shrimp with heads and tails is the best source of shells; another option is keeping a bag in your freezer and adding discards from other recipes over time.

- **2 pounds (906 g) shrimp**

- **2 tablespoons olive oil, divided**

- **2 cups (240 g) celery, chopped & divided**

- **2 cups (288 g) onion, chopped & divided**

- **1 cup (160 g) carrots, chopped**

- **4 teaspoons salt, divided**

- **2 garlic cloves, smashed**

- **2 teaspoons thyme, divided**

- **1 teaspoon black peppercorns**

- **12 cups (2.8 L) water, divided**

- **10 bay leaves, divided**

- **4 cups (500 g) okra, sliced**

- **2 cups (280 g) tomatoes, chopped**

- **½ teaspoon cayenne pepper**

Peel and refrigerate shrimp, reserving shells.

Over medium heat, warm a large stockpot.

Add one tablespoon olive oil, reserved shrimp shells, one cup (120 g) celery, one cup (144 g) onion, carrots, 2 teaspoons salt, garlic, one teaspoon thyme and peppercorns, sautéing several minutes.

Add 8 cups water and 4 bay leaves, simmering for 15 minutes.

Remove from heat.

Drain broth in a fine-mesh strainer, set aside.

Discard solids.

Over medium heat, rewarm stockpot.

Add remaining olive oil and okra, sautéing for 10 minutes.

Add tomatoes, remaining celery and onions, sautéing, until tender.

Add reserved shrimp broth, remaining water, salt, thyme, bay leaves and cayenne pepper, stirring, until combined.

Increase heat to medium-high, bringing broth to a rolling boil.

Decrease heat to low, simmering for 45 minutes.

Add shrimp, stirring occasionally for 10 minutes.

Discard bay leaves and serve.

Yield: 10 | Serving Size: 1 cup
Calories: 162   Net Carbs: 14g   Total Carbs: 18g   Fat: 7g   Protein: 9g   Fiber: 4g

Minestrone *with* Parmesan

An Italian culinary classic, this minestrone recipe is anything but traditional. Don't let the long list of ingredients put you off, they meld together and create a savory vegetable soup with a surprise umami back note.

- 2 tablespoons olive oil
- 2 cups (288 g) onion, chopped
- 6 teaspoons garlic, minced
- 4 cups (560 g) tomatoes, chopped
- 1 cup (160 g) carrots, sliced
- ½ cup (40 g) red pepper, finely chopped
- 1 cup (70 g) cabbage, shredded
- ½ cup (60 g) celery, chopped
- 4 cups (946 ml) low-sodium vegetable stock
- ⅓ cup (79 ml) reduced-sodium tamari
- 1 tablespoon thyme, minced
- 1 teaspoon oregano
- 2 bay leaves
- 2 cups (130 g) broccoli, chopped
- 2 cups (300 g) edamame
- 2 cups (300 g) zucchini, sliced
- 1 cup (30 g) parsley, chopped
- 2 teaspoons salt
- 1 teaspoon black pepper
- 1 cup (40 g) Parmesan cheese, grated

Over medium heat, warm a large stockpot.

Add olive oil, onion and garlic, sautéing, until tender.

Add tomatoes, carrots and red pepper, sautéing, for 5 minutes.

Add cabbage and celery, sautéing, for 5 minutes.

Add stock, tamari, thyme, oregano and bay leaves, stirring, until combined.

Cover pot and decrease heat to low, simmering for 45 minutes.

Add broccoli, edamame, zucchini, parsley, salt and pepper, simmering for 10 minutes.

Discard bay leaves.

Top with Parmesan cheese and serve.

Fish Stew with Tomato & Saffron

Aromatic, sweet saffron is the shining star of this simple fish stew inspired by traditional Portuguese Caldeirada. Firm halibut and sea bass balance the light, richly flavored tomato broth, while keeping their meaty texture as they simmer.

- ¼ teaspoon saffron, crushed
- 2 tablespoons boiling water
- 3 tablespoons olive oil, divided
- 2 teaspoons thyme, minced
- 1 teaspoon lemon zest
- 2 teaspoons salt, divided
- ⅛ teaspoon black pepper
- 1 pound (454 g) halibut fillet
- 1 pound (454 g) sea bass fillet
- 2 cups (288 g) onion, chopped
- 4 teaspoons garlic, minced
- ½ teaspoon fennel seed, crushed
- ½ teaspoon red chili flakes
- 1 bay leaf
- 3 cups (710 ml) water
- 1 cup (237 ml) dry white wine
- 2 cups (280 g) tomatoes, chopped

- 2 tablespoons tomato paste
- ¼ cup (8 g) parsley, minced
- 1 tablespoon lemon juice

In a small bowl, combine saffron and boiling water, set aside.

In a large bowl, add 2 tablespoons olive oil, one teaspoon thyme, lemon zest, ½ teaspoon salt and pepper, stirring, until combined.

Cut fish fillets into 2-inch pieces.

Add fish to marinade, tossing to coat.

Set aside.

Over medium heat, warm a large stockpot.

Add remaining olive oil and onion, sautéing, until tender.

Add remaining thyme and salt, saffron tea, garlic, fennel seed, red chili flakes and bay leaf, stirring, until combined.

Add water, wine, tomatoes and tomato paste, stirring, until combined.

Cover pot and decrease heat to low, simmering for 30 minutes.

Add fish and parsley to broth, simmering, until fish flakes easily.

Discard bay leaf.

Top with lemon juice and serve immediately.

Yield: 6 | Serving Size: 1 cup
Calories: 278   Net Carbs: 8g   Total Carbs: 10g   Fat: 10g   Protein: 29g   Fiber: 2g

Yield: 6 | Serving Size: 1 cup

Calories: 60   Net Carbs: 7g   Total Carbs: 9g   Fat: 3g   Protein: 2g   Fiber: 2g

Curry Cauliflower Soup

This soup is a comfort on a cold day—warm, hearty with an earthy, curry back note. Low in carbohydrate cauliflower blends into a creamy consistency, while golden turmeric reminds me of summer sun.

Please note you will need an immersion blender for this recipe.

- **1 tablespoon olive oil**

- **1 cup (144 g) onion, chopped**

- **2 teaspoons garlic, minced**

- **2 teaspoons curry powder**

- **½ teaspoon black pepper**

- **¼ teaspoon turmeric**

- **4 cups (540 g) cauliflower, cored & chopped**

- **4 cups (946 ml) low-sodium vegetable stock**

- **2 teaspoons salt**

- **¼ cup (5 g) cilantro, finely chopped**

Over medium heat, warm a large stockpot.

Add olive oil and onion, sautéing, until tender.

Add garlic, stirring, until fragrant.

Add curry powder, pepper and turmeric, stirring, until fragrant.

Add cauliflower, stock and salt, stirring, until combined.

Increase heat to medium-high, bringing soup to a rolling boil.

Cover pot and decrease heat to low, simmering for 30 minutes.

Using an immersion blender, purée soup, until smooth.

Top with cilantro and serve.

Yield: 8 | Serving Size: 1 cup

Calories: 219   Net Carbs: 5g   Total Carbs: 6g   Fat: 14g   Protein: 17g   Fiber: 1g

Chicken Soup

Nothing is more comforting than chicken soup when you're feeling under the weather. This almost classic recipe relies on savory rosemary for an unexpected twist. I prefer dark chicken thighs for flavor and their ability to withstand a long simmer.

- 2 pounds (906 g) bone-in chicken thighs
- 2 cups (473 ml) boiling water
- ½ tablespoon chicken bouillon
- 1 tablespoon olive oil
- 1 tablespoon garlic, minced
- 1 cup (160 g) carrots, chopped
- 1 cup (120 g) celery, chopped
- 1 cup (120 g) leeks, sliced
- 4 cups (946 ml) low-sodium chicken broth
- ½ cup (15 g) parsley, chopped
- 1½ teaspoons salt
- ½ teaspoon rosemary
- ¼ teaspoon black pepper
- 3 bay leaves

Rinse chicken and pat dry, set aside.

In a small bowl, add boiling water and bouillon, whisking, until combined.

Set aside.

Over medium heat, warm a large stockpot.

Add olive oil and garlic, stirring, until fragrant.

Add carrot, celery and leeks, sautéing, until tender.

Add chicken, bouillon water, broth, parsley, salt, rosemary, pepper and bay leaves.

Increase heat to medium-high, bringing soup to a rolling boil.

Cover pot and decrease heat to low, simmering for 45 minutes.

Remove chicken, debone and rough chop.

Discard bones and bay leaves.

Add chicken to soup and serve.

Yield: 8 | Serving Size: 1 cup
Calories: 115   Net Carbs: 11g   Total Carbs: 15g   Fat: 4g   Protein: 4g   Fiber: 4g

White Vegetable Soup

High-fiber, low in carbohydrate vegetables balance out starchy cannellini beans in this creamy, hearty soup with a spicy red pepper finish. Dry white wine adds a touch of acidity, while the roasted cauliflower topping lends just a touch of sweetness.

Please note you will need an immersion blender for this recipe.

- **5 cups (675 g) cauliflower florets, divided**
- **2 tablespoons olive oil, divided**
- **1 cup (144 g) onion, chopped**
- **1 tablespoon garlic, minced**
- **1 cup (125 g) celeriac, peeled & chopped**
- **1 cup (125 g) turnips, peeled & chopped**
- **½ cup (118 ml) dry white wine**
- **1½ teaspoons salt**
- **4 cups (946 ml) low-sodium vegetable stock**
- **1 cup (200 g) cannellini beans**
- **½ teaspoon black pepper**
- **½ teaspoon thyme**
- **¼ teaspoon red chili flakes**

Preheat oven to 375°F.

Line a rimmed baking sheet with parchment.

Arrange one cup (135 g) cauliflower florets on prepared sheet.

Brush with one tablespoon olive oil.

Roast for 20 minutes, until golden brown and tender.

Rough chop roasted cauliflower and set aside.

Over medium heat, warm a large stockpot.

Add remaining olive oil, onion and garlic, sautéing, until tender.

Add remaining cauliflower, celeriac, turnips, wine and salt, stirring, until combined.

Cover pot and decrease heat to low, simmering for 10 minutes.

Add stock, beans, pepper, thyme and red chili flakes.

Increase heat to medium-high, bringing soup to a rolling boil.

Cover pot and decrease heat to low, simmering for 30 minutes.

Using an immersion blender, purée soup, until smooth.

Top with chopped roasted cauliflower and serve.

Sides

A great meal is all about flavor and depth. Sides provide complimentary punch and pizzazz—not only in terms of extra nutrients and fiber, but also texture and variety.

I've included recipes to target all five food flavors—sweet, sour, salty, slightly bitter and savory. Swapping traditional carbohydrate laden standards with complex, layered alternatives to elevate your offerings, while keeping your blood sugar stable.

Yield: 6 | Serving Size: 1 cup

Calories: 253   Net Carbs: 11g   Total Carbs: 15g   Fat: 20g   Protein: 5g   Fiber: 4g

Roasted Carrots *with* Chimichurri & Feta

Carrots show their sweet spot when roasted, contrasting nicely against herby, punchy, slightly spicy chimichurri. Traditionally a South American condiment, this sauce is best served fresh, so I recommend waiting until the carrots are almost ready to pull from the oven before finishing the final steps.

Please note you will need a food processor for this recipe.

- **6 cups (960 g) carrots, halved lengthwise**
- **1 tablespoon olive oil**
- **¼ cup (59 ml) red wine vinegar**
- **1 tablespoon jalapeño, seeded & minced**
- **1 tablespoon shallots, minced**
- **2 teaspoons garlic, minced**
- **1 teaspoon salt**
- **½ cup (10 g) cilantro, chopped**
- **⅛ cup (3 g) oregano, chopped**
- **⅛ cup (4 g) parsley, chopped**
- **⅓ cup (79 ml) extra-virgin olive oil**
- **1 cup (120 g) feta, crumbled**

Preheat oven to 425°F.

Line a rimmed baking sheet with parchment.

Arrange carrots on prepared sheet.

Brush carrots with olive oil.

Roast for 30 minutes, until tender.

Using a processor, blend vinegar, jalapeño, shallots, garlic and salt, until combined.

Rest for 5 minutes.

Add cilantro, oregano and parsley, pulsing, until combined and textured.

Add extra-virgin olive oil in parts, pulsing, until well-combined.

Drizzle chimichurri over warm, roasted carrots.

Top with feta and serve.

Baked Eggplant *with* Marinara, Parmesan & Goat Cheese

Inspired by eggplant Parmigiana but elevated with punchy sun-dried tomato marinara and tangy goat cheese, this simplified recipe omits breadcrumbs and passes on the pan-fry in favor of oven-baking. A largely hands-off meal, it's best made in late eggplant season when the autumn weather turns chilly.

- 8 cups (680 g) eggplant, sliced in ¼-inch rounds

- 2 tablespoons olive oil

- ¾ cup (177 ml) sun-dried tomato marinara

- 1 cup (30 g) basil leaves

- 1 cup (120 g) goat cheese, crumbled

- 1 cup (40 g) Parmesan cheese, grated

- ½ cup (20 g) Parmesan cheese, shaved

Preheat oven to 400°F.

Line several rimmed baking sheets with parchment.

Arrange eggplant in a single layer on prepared sheets.

Brush eggplant with olive oil.

Roast for 20 minutes, until tender.

In a large casserole dish, arrange half the roasted eggplant in a single layer.

Spread ⅓ cup (79 ml) marinara over first eggplant layer.

Add ½ cup (15 g) basil, ½ cup (60 g) goat cheese and ½ cup (40 g) grated Parmesan.

Repeat for an additional layer.

Top with ½ cup (20 g) shaved Parmesan.

Cover, baking for 30 minutes.

Remove cover, baking for 10 additional minutes.

Rest for 10 minutes before serving.

For Good Measure: A Diabetic Cookbook

Sun-Dried Tomato Marinara

Please note you will need a food processor for this recipe.

- **1 cup (140 g) tomatoes, chopped**

- **¼ cup (19 g) sun-dried tomatoes**

- **¼ cup (8 g) basil**

- **2 tablespoons parsley, minced**

- **1 tablespoon red onion, minced**

- **½ tablespoon extra-virgin olive oil**

- **½ teaspoon garlic, minced**

- **¼ teaspoon apple cider vinegar**

- **¼ teaspoon red chili flakes**

- **¼ teaspoon maple syrup**

- **¼ teaspoon oregano**

- **⅛ teaspoon black pepper**

- **⅛ teaspoon salt**

Using a processor, blend tomatoes, sun-dried tomatoes, basil, parsley, red onion, extra-virgin olive oil, garlic, vinegar, red chili flakes, maple syrup, oregano, pepper and salt, until thick and creamy.

Store refrigerated in a sealed, glass container.

Yield: 8 | Serving Size: 1 cup

Calories: 228   Net Carbs: 7g   Total Carbs: 10g   Fat: 16g   Protein: 12g   Fiber: 3g

Yield: 6 | Serving Size: ½ cup

Calories: 46   Net Carbs: 5g   Total Carbs: 6g   Fat: 2g   Protein: 1g   Fiber: 1g

Fresh Kimchi

Inspired in flavor by traditional Korean cabbage kimchi, this simplified version relies on a warm, salt and sugar brine to quickly soften the napa cabbage and add flavor, while garlic, ginger, and spicy gochugaru add authenticity to this crisp, intensely seasoned side dish.

- **4 cups (160 g) napa cabbage, chopped**

- **4 cups (946 ml) water**

- **2 tablespoons salt**

- **2 tablespoons sugar**

- **1 tablespoon toasted sesame oil**

- **1 teaspoon garlic, minced**

- **1 teaspoon ginger, minced**

- **1 teaspoon gochugaru**

In a large bowl, add cabbage, set aside.

Over low heat, warm a small saucepan.

Add water, salt and sugar, stirring, until salt dissolves.

Pour brine over cabbage, submerging leaves.

Rest for 30 minutes.

Drain and rinse cabbage, set aside.

In a small bowl, add sesame oil, garlic, ginger and gochugaru, stirring, until combined.

Pour seasoned oil mixture over cabbage, tossing, until well-coated.

Rest for 30 minutes before serving.

Yield: 6 | Serving Size: 1 cup + ¼ cup romesco

Calories: 219   Net Carbs: 6g   Total Carbs: 11g   Fat: 19g   Protein: 5g   Fiber: 5g

Roasted Spiced Cauliflower
with **Romesco**

A powerful spice blend ramps up the flavor in this versatile side. Red wine vinegar adds an unexpected back note, while earthly, slightly smoky yet sweet, romesco finishes it off. This dish is great alongside a hearty main or on its own as a crowd-pleasing starter.

- **7 cups (945 g) cauliflower florets**
- **¼ cup (57 g) butter, melted**
- **1 tablespoon paprika**
- **1 teaspoon curry powder**
- **½ teaspoon coriander**
- **½ teaspoon cumin**
- **½ teaspoon salt**
- **⅛ teaspoon black pepper**
- **2 tablespoons red wine vinegar**
- **1½ cups (420 g) romesco (see page 71)**

Preheat oven to 375°F.

Line a rimmed baking sheet with parchment.

Arrange cauliflower in a single layer on prepared sheet.

Brush cauliflower with butter.

In a small bowl, add paprika, curry powder, coriander, cumin, salt and pepper, stirring, until combined.

Sprinkle spice mixture over cauliflower, until evenly coated.

Roast for 20 minutes, until tender.

Drizzle vinegar over warm, roasted cauliflower.

Serve warm with romesco.

Yield: 8 | Serving Size: ½ cup

Calories: 80   Net Carbs: 11g   Total Carbs: 13g   Fat: 4g   Protein: 1g   Fiber: 2g

Roasted Butternut Squash *with* Apple & Thyme

Sweet and savory, this autumnal dish is perfect alongside a hearty main for a seasonal meal. While butternut squash skin is edible, it can be tough and textured. I highly recommend peeling. Trim the ends to create a study base and use a vegetable peeler to make quick work of the task.

- **4 cups (560 g) butternut squash, peeled & cubed**

- **2 tablespoons olive oil, divided**

- **½ teaspoon sea salt**

- **2 cups (260 g) Granny Smith apples, cubed**

- **½ teaspoon thyme**

- **1 tablespoon fresh thyme, minced**

Preheat oven to 350°F.

Line a rimmed baking sheet with parchment.

Arrange squash in a single layer on prepared sheet.

Brush squash with one tablespoon olive oil and sprinkle with sea salt.

Cover with aluminum foil, roasting 30 minutes.

In a small bowl, add remaining olive oil, apples and thyme, tossing, until well-coated.

Remove foil cover from squash.

Add apple mixture, roasting uncovered 20 additional minutes, until tender.

Top with fresh thyme and serve warm.

Yield: 8 | Serving Size: 1 cup

Calories: 257 Net Carbs: 7g Total Carbs: 12g Fat: 20g Protein: 10g Fiber: 5g

Cauliflower Gratin

Think of this gratin as elevated macaroni and cheese. Nestled in a nest of spicy wilted kale, cauliflower absorbs butter and flavor as it slow roasts to a tender, creamy texture. Rich, decadent and comforting on a cold, winter day.

- 6 cups (810 g) cauliflower florets
- 2 tablespoons butter
- ½ cup (60 g) leeks, sliced
- 3 tablespoons garlic, minced
- 1½ teaspoons sea salt, divided
- 8 cups (200 g) kale, chopped
- ½ teaspoon red chili flakes
- 1 tablespoon thyme
- 1½ cups (60 g) Parmesan cheese, grated & divided
- 1 cup (236 ml) heavy cream

Preheat oven to 400°F.

In a large casserole dish, arrange cauliflower in a single layer, set aside.

Over medium heat, warm a nonstick skillet.

Add butter to heated pan.

Add leeks, garlic and ½ teaspoon salt, sautéing, until leeks are golden.

Add kale, red chili flakes and thyme, stirring, until kale is slightly wilted.

Distribute wilted kale mixture over cauliflower.

Over medium heat, rewarm the nonstick skillet.

Add one cup (40 g) Parmesan, heavy cream and remaining salt, stirring, until cheese is melted.

Pour cream mixture over cauliflower and kale.

Top with remaining Parmesan.

Cover with aluminum foil, baking 20 minutes.

Remove foil cover, baking uncovered 20 additional minutes, until tender.

Serve warm.

Yield: 6 | Serving Size: 2 blossoms + 2 tablespoons marinara

Calories: 231   Net Carbs: 6g   Total Carbs: 8g   Fat: 18g   Protein: 11g   Fiber: 2g

Ricotta-Stuffed Zucchini Blossoms *with* Sun-Dried Tomato Marinara

Inspired by an Italian classic, we substituted almond flour for wheat and opted to pan-sear to keep the breading in place. Under quick heat, the ricotta and mozzarella melt into creamy richness and the almond flour turns golden—the perfect base for zingy, sun-dried tomato marinara. Vibrant, yellow zucchini blooms dot farmstands in mid to late summer and are sometimes found at specialty grocers throughout the year.

- 1 cup (232 g) ricotta cheese
- ¼ cup (55 g) mozzarella, grated
- ¼ cup (12 g) chives, minced
- ½ teaspoon salt, divided
- ⅛ teaspoon black pepper
- 12 zucchini blossoms
- 2 eggs
- ½ cup (55 g) almond flour
- 2 tablespoons olive oil
- ¾ cup (177 ml) sun-dried tomato marinara (see page 109)

In a small bowl, add ricotta, mozzarella, chives, ¼ teaspoon salt and pepper, stirring, until combined.

Using a small spoon, fill each blossom with 2 tablespoons of cheese mixture, twisting ends to secure.

In a small bowl, whisk eggs until slightly frothy, set aside.

In a separate small bowl, add remaining salt and almond flour, stirring, until combined.

Set aside.

Over medium heat, warm a nonstick skillet.

Add olive oil to heated pan.

Dip each stuffed blossom into whisked eggs, dredge in almond flour mixture, and place in heated skillet.

Cook for 8 minutes, flipping hallway through, until golden.

Serve warm with sun-dried tomato marinara.

Yield: 8 | Serving Size: ½ cup
Calories: 74 Net Carbs: 9g Total Carbs: 12g Fat: 2g Protein: 2g Fiber: 3g

Quick Sauerkraut

Purists would argue this purple cabbage is not classic sauerkraut as it is not fermented. The counterargument agrees but points out it comes together quickly in less than an hour. Bold, crisp and slightly sour flavors pair with caraway seeds for authenticity, making this recipe a perfect topping to your favorite sandwich or wherever else you crave a pickled side.

- 1¼ cup (296 ml) apple cider vinegar

- ¾ cup (177 ml) water

- 1 tablespoon salt

- 1 teaspoon caraway seeds

- 1 cup (144 g) onion, sliced

- 1 tablespoon olive oil

- 12 cups (840 g) purple cabbage, finely sliced

In a small bowl, add vinegar, water, salt and caraway seeds, stirring, until combined.

Set aside.

Over medium heat, warm a large stockpot.

Add onion and olive oil, sautéing, until tender.

Add cabbage and vinegar mixture.

Increase heat to medium-high, bringing to a rolling boil.

Cover pot and decrease heat to low, simmering for 45 minutes.

Serve warm.

Yield: 6 | Serving Size: 1 cup + ¼ cup tzatziki

Calories: 107 Net Carbs: 4g Total Carbs: 7g Fat: 7g Protein: 4g Fiber: 3g

Roasted Eggplant *with* Tzatziki

Brushed with herby, tangy sumac and za'atar, creamy, roasted eggplant is served alongside cool, refreshing tzatziki. While incredibly simple to prepare, tzatziki demands highly drained, grated cucumber or it will separate. After all the options I've tried, clean hands are still the best tool for the job.

- 1 cup (120 g) cucumber, seeded & grated
- 1 cup (260 g) plain Greek yogurt
- 1 tablespoon extra-virgin olive oil
- 1 teaspoon garlic, minced
- ¼ teaspoon salt
- ¼ teaspoon red wine vinegar
- ⅛ teaspoon black pepper
- 6 cups (510 g) eggplant, sliced in ¼-inch rounds
- 2 teaspoons sumac
- 2 teaspoons za'atar
- 1 teaspoon sea salt
- 2 tablespoons olive oil

Squeeze grated cucumber to remove excess moisture, set aside.

In a small bowl, add yogurt, whisking, until smooth and creamy.

Add well-drained cucumber, extra-virgin olive oil, garlic, salt, vinegar and pepper, stirring, until well-combined.

Refrigerate until serving.

Preheat oven to 400°F.

Line several rimmed baking sheets with parchment.

Arrange eggplant in a single layer on prepared sheets.

In a small bowl, add sumac, za'atar and sea salt, stirring, until combined.

Brush eggplant with olive oil and sprinkle with spice mixture.

Roast for 20 minutes, until golden brown and tender.

Serve warm with tzatziki.

Mains

Sunset is a profound moment over the Pacific Ocean—always interesting, almost never the same. After hours of harsh light, quiet darkness is warmly welcomed. The moon rises and the day's energy gives way to comfort, as we gather to reflect and nourish.

Is tonight's meal casual? Or are you inviting guests into the dining room? Do you need to balance your blood sugar? Are you hoping to expand your skills with something layered and complex or do you want to rely on the slow cooker to do the work for you?

The recipes in this section offer plenty of options. The ideal meal is a balance and while many pair well with a layered salad or side dish, most are perfectly complemented by simple conversation.

Yield: 8 | Serving Size: 4 ounces (113 g)
Calories: 130   Net Carbs: 0g   Total Carbs: 1g   Fat: 3g   Protein: 24g   Fiber: 1g

Slow-Cooked Balsamic Chicken

Balsamic vinegar creates incredibly flavorful, juicy and tender chicken. Entirely hands-off except for a quick prep, this is my favorite go-to weeknight meal with the bonus of leftovers. The herby crust keeps it interesting and if you prefer dark meat, chicken thighs are an easy substitution.

Please note you will need a slow cooker for this recipe.

- **½ cup (118 ml) low-sodium chicken broth**
- **½ cup (118 ml) balsamic vinegar**
- **2 tablespoons brown sugar**
- **4 teaspoons garlic, minced**
- **1 teaspoon basil**
- **1 teaspoon sea salt**
- **½ teaspoon oregano**
- **½ teaspoon rosemary**
- **½ teaspoon thyme**
- **¼ teaspoon black pepper**
- **¼ teaspoon red chili flakes**
- **2 pounds (907 g) boneless chicken breast**

In a small bowl, add chicken broth, vinegar, brown sugar and garlic, whisking, until combined.

In a separate small bowl, add basil, salt, oregano, rosemary, thyme, black pepper and red chili flakes, stirring, until combined.

Set aside.

Arrange chicken in a single layer in the crock of the slow cooker.

Pour vinegar mixture over chicken.

Sprinkle herb mixture over chicken, until a crust-like coating is formed.

Cook covered on low for 6 hours or until internal temperature reaches 165 degrees.

Remove chicken from juices and serve.

Slow-Cooked Moroccan Chicken Stew *with* Saffron Cauliflower Rice

Fragrant with ginger, cumin, and coriander, shredded chicken layers with sweet, saffron cauliflower rice for an incredibly flavorful meal. Don't let the long list of ingredients and instructions deter you, they come together simply with your slow cooker doing the bulk of the work. Using a food processor to finely chop the cauliflower works as a quick substitute for hand grating.

Please note you will need a slow cooker for this recipe.

- **2 pounds (907 g) boneless chicken thighs**
- **2 teaspoons salt**
- **½ teaspoon saffron, crushed & divided**
- **2 tablespoons boiling water, divided**
- **¼ cup (5 g) cilantro, chopped**
- **4 teaspoons garlic, minced**
- **1 tablespoon ginger, minced**
- **1 tablespoon lemon zest**
- **1 teaspoon coriander**
- **1 teaspoon cumin**
- **1 teaspoon paprika**
- **1 cup (237 ml) low-sodium chicken broth**

- **1 tablespoon olive oil**
- **2 cups (288 g) onion, sliced**
- **½ cup (80 g) Castelvetrano olives, pitted & halved**
- **¼ cup (57 g) butter**
- **2 teaspoons cumin seeds**
- **8 cups (1.1 kg) cauliflower, grated**
- **2 teaspoons sea salt**
- **2 tablespoons lemon juice**

~~~~~~~~~~~~~~~~~~~~~~~~

In a large bowl, add chicken and salt, tossing, until combined.

In a small bowl, combine ¼ teaspoon saffron and one tablespoon boiling water, set aside.

In a separate small bowl, add cilantro, garlic, ginger, lemon zest, coriander, cumin and paprika, stirring, until combined.

Add spice mixture to salted chicken, tossing, until combined.

Add chicken broth and olive oil to saffron mixture, stirring, until combined.

Arrange onions in a single layer in the crock of the slow cooker.

Pour broth mixture over onions.

Nestle chicken in a single layer amid onions and broth.

Sprinkle with olives.

Cook covered on low for 4 hours or until internal temperature reaches 165 degrees.

With 20 minutes remaining on slow cooker...

In a small bowl, combine remaining saffron and boiling water, set aside.

Over medium heat, warm a large, nonstick skillet.

Add butter to heated pan, stirring, until melted.

Add cumin seeds, stirring for one minute, until fragrant.

Add cauliflower, sautéing, until tender.

Add saffron water and sea salt, stirring, until combined.

Remove from heat.

Shred chicken in juices and add lemon juice.

Serve over warm saffron cauliflower rice.

Yield: 8 | Serving Size: 4 ounces (113 g) chicken + ½ cup cauliflower rice
Calories: 396 Net Carbs: 9g Total Carbs: 14g Fat: 29g Protein: 23g Fiber: 5g

Crispy Chicken Tacos

Inspired by beach town taquerias, this chicken taco holds its own. Marinated in a blend of bright California citrus and pan-fried with caramelized onions, it's served on a soft tortilla layered with crunchy cabbage, creamy avocado and sharp cheddar. Leftover chicken works great here or in a pinch, you can substitute a grocery-store rotisserie.

Please note you will need a food processor for this recipe.

- ½ cup (118 ml) orange juice
- ⅛ cup (59 ml) lemon juice
- ⅛ cup (59 ml) lime juice
- 3 cups (450 g) cooked chicken, shredded
- 1 teaspoon salt
- ½ teaspoon black pepper
- 1 cup (110 g) almond flour
- 3 tablespoons coconut flour
- 2 teaspoons xanthan gum
- 1 teaspoon baking powder
- ½ teaspoon sea salt
- 1 tablespoon water
- 2 teaspoons apple cider vinegar
- 1 egg
- 3 tablespoons butter
- 2 cups (288 g) onion, sliced

- ¾ cup (53 g) purple cabbage, shredded
- ¾ cup (150 g) avocado, sliced
- ⅓ cup (43 g) cheddar, grated

~~~~~~~~~~~~~~~~~~~~~~~~~~~~~~~~

In a large, nonreactive bowl, add orange, lemon and lime juices, stirring, until combined.

Add chicken, salt and pepper, tossing, until combined.

Set aside to marinate.

Using a processor, blend almond flour, coconut flour, xanthan gum, baking powder and sea salt, until combined.

Add water, vinegar and egg, pulsing, until dough comes together.

Divide dough into six pieces, rolling each into a ball, set aside.

Over medium heat, warm a large, nonstick skillet.

Add butter to heated pan, stirring, until melted.

Add onions, sautéing, until golden brown and transparent.

Add chicken and juices, sautéing, until brown and crispy.

Remove from heat.

Over medium heat, warm a small, nonstick skillet.

Using a rolling pin, flatten each dough ball between parchment.

Add to heated skillet, cooking for one minute.

Flip, cooking an additional minute, until golden brown.

Repeat with remaining dough.

Fill each with ½ cup (approximately 75 g) crispy chicken, 2 tablespoons shredded cabbage, 2 tablespoons avocado and one tablespoon cheddar.

Serve immediately.

Yield: 6 | Serving Size: 1 taco

Calories: 396   Net Carbs: 12g   Total Carbs: 18g   Fat: 29g   Protein: 19g   Fiber: 6g

Chicken Satays *with* Peanut Sauce

These fragrant curry-spiced skewers of tender, grilled chicken are slathered in a rich peanut sauce. A play on a classic Malaysian street food, satays are great as a main course alongside a crispy salad or as a crowd-pleasing appetizer. If you forget to soak the bamboo, substitute metal skewers, or keep it simple and grill the marinated chicken in pieces.

- 8 bamboo skewers

- 2 pounds (907 g) boneless, skinless chicken thighs

- 2 tablespoons lemongrass, sliced

- 2 tablespoons lemon juice

- 2 tablespoons brown sugar

- 2 tablespoons reduced-sodium tamari

- 1 tablespoon coriander

- 1 tablespoon garlic, minced

- 1 tablespoon ginger, minced

- 2 teaspoons curry powder

- ¼ teaspoon cumin

- ½ cup (144 g) peanut sauce

Fill a large bowl with water, submerge bamboo skewers, set aside.

Trim chicken thighs into 1-ounce, 1-inch cubes.

In a large, shallow pan, add lemongrass, lemon juice, brown sugar, tamari, coriander, garlic, ginger, curry and cumin, stirring, until combined.

Set aside.

Spear four pieces of chicken on each skewer.

Add skewered chicken to marinade, tossing, until coated.

Cover and refrigerate for 2 hours.

Preheat grill to medium-high.

Remove chicken skewers from marinade.

Grill, flipping once, until slightly charred and internal temperature reaches 165 degrees.

Serve warm with peanut sauce.

Peanut Sauce

Please note you will need a food processor for this recipe

- ½ cup (140 g) peanut butter

- 2 tablespoons rice vinegar

- 2 tablespoons boiling water

- 1 tablespoon reduced-sodium tamari

- 1 teaspoon honey

Using a processor, blend peanut butter, vinegar, water, tamari and honey, until well-combined.

Store refrigerated in a sealed, glass container.

Yield: 8 | Serving Size: 1 skewer + 1 tablespoon peanut sauce
Calories: 343   Net Carbs: 3g   Total Carbs: 4g   Fat: 25g   Protein: 25g   Fiber: 1g

Yield: 12 | Serving Size: 1 lettuce cup

Calories: 110   Net Carbs: 5g   Total Carbs: 7g   Fat: 6g   Protein: 8g   Fiber: 2g

Hoisin Chicken Lettuce Cups

Crisp, fresh and bright with an umami kick from the sweet and salty hoisin sauce, these lettuce cups are a perfect light meal on a warm evening or fun finger food for your next gathering. Delicate bib lettuce wilts fast, so keep everything deconstructed until you are ready to serve.

- 1 tablespoon olive oil

- 1 pound (454 g) chicken, ground

- 1 cup (144 g) onion, finely chopped

- 1 tablespoon ginger, minced

- 2 teaspoons garlic, minced

- ¼ cup (59 ml) hoisin sauce

- 2 tablespoons reduced-sodium tamari

- 1 tablespoon rice vinegar

- ½ cup (130 g) water chestnuts, drained & finely chopped

- 24 bib lettuce leaves

- ¾ cup (150 g) avocado, smashed

Over medium heat, warm a large, nonstick skillet.

Add olive oil to heated pan.

Add chicken, onion, ginger and garlic, sautéing, until golden brown.

In a small bowl, add hoisin, tamari and vinegar, whisking, until well-combined.

Add hoisin mixture and water chestnuts to chicken, stirring, until combined.

Remove from heat.

Arrange lettuce leaves creating twelve cups.

Spoon 4 tablespoons hoisin chicken into each lettuce cup.

Top with one tablespoon avocado.

Serve immediately.

Turkey Meatballs *with* Marinara

Dark ground turkey adds a richness to these savory meatballs flavored with a hint of Parmesan cheese and thyme. Simmered in a soffritto-based, classic tomato marinara, they are perfect alone or served on a bed of wilted dark leafy greens or zucchini noodles. Marinara is best simmered slow over low heat allowing the tomatoes to reduce and their flavor to intensify.

Please note you will need a food processor for this recipe.

- **6 cups (840 g) tomatoes, chopped**
- **2 tablespoons olive oil, divided**
- **1 cup (144 g) onion, finely chopped**
- **½ cup (80 g) carrots, finely chopped**
- **½ cup (60 g) celery, finely chopped**
- **1 teaspoon salt**
- **1 teaspoon black pepper, divided**
- **3 bay leaves**
- **½ cup (15 g) basil, chopped**
- **2 tablespoons butter**
- **1 pound (454 g) dark turkey meat, ground**
- **½ cup (116 g) ricotta cheese**
- **½ cup (20 g) Parmesan cheese, grated & divided**

- **1 tablespoon thyme, minced**
- **1 teaspoon granulated onion**
- **½ teaspoon sea salt**

Using a processor, add tomatoes, pulsing, until puréed.

Set aside.

Over medium heat, warm a large stockpot.

Add one tablespoon olive oil, onion, carrots and celery, sautéing, until tender.

Add puréed tomatoes, salt, ½ teaspoon pepper and bay leaves, stirring, until combined.

Cover pot and decrease heat to low, simmering for 4 hours.

With 20 minutes remaining on sauce, remove lid and bay leaves.

Add basil and butter, stirring, until combined.

In a large bowl, add turkey, ricotta, ¼ cup (10 g) Parmesan, thyme, granulated onion, sea salt and remaining pepper, stirring, until well-combined.

Using a tablespoon, divide turkey mixture into eighteen parts.

Roll each into a ball, set aside.

Over medium heat, warm a large, nonstick skillet.

Add remaining olive oil to heated pan, swirling to thinly coat bottom.

Add turkey meatballs to pan, sautéing, until browned.

Add marinara to skillet, simmering for an additional 20 minutes.

Top with remaining Parmesan and serve.

Yield: 6 | Serving Size: 3 turkey meatballs + ½ cup marinara

Calories: 277   Net Carbs: 9g   Total Carbs: 12g   Fat: 15g   Protein: 24g   Fiber: 3g

Apple Turkey Burgers *with* Flaxseed Buns

Apple adds an unexpected twist to the classic turkey burger. Moist, textured and full of flavor, they're best topped with your favorite fixings and sandwiched between fluffy, nutty flaxseed buns for an elevated, somewhat autumnal, version of burger night.

- 2 cups (200 g) flaxseed meal
- 2 teaspoons baking soda
- 2 teaspoons salt, divided
- 1 teaspoon caraway seeds
- ½ teaspoon black pepper, divided
- ⅓ cup (76 g) butter, melted
- ¼ cup (59 ml) apple cider vinegar
- 1 tablespoon maple syrup
- 6 eggs, beaten
- 2 tablespoons olive oil, divided
- ½ cup (60 g) celery, finely chopped
- ½ cup (24 g) scallions, finely sliced
- 2 teaspoons garlic, minced
- 1 pound (454 g) turkey, ground
- ½ cup (65 g) Granny Smith apple, grated
- 1 tablespoon chives, chopped

- 1 tablespoon thyme, minced
- 2 teaspoons sesame seeds

Preheat oven to 400°F.

Line two rimmed baking sheets with parchment.

In a large bowl, add flaxseed meal, baking soda, one teaspoon salt, caraway seeds and ¼ teaspoon pepper, stirring, until well-combined.

In a small bowl, add butter, vinegar, syrup and eggs, stirring, until well-combined.

Add butter mixture to flax mixture, stirring, until well-combined.

Rest for 10 minutes.

Over medium heat, warm a small, nonstick skillet.

Add one tablespoon olive oil, celery, scallions and garlic, sautéing, until tender.

In a large bowl, add turkey, apple, chives, thyme, remaining salt and pepper, stirring, until well-combined.

Add celery mixture, stirring, until well-combined.

Using a ⅓ cup, divide turkey mixture into six parts.

Flatten and shape into patties.

Set aside.

Using a ¼-cup measure, scoop rested flax mixture onto prepared baking sheets in twelve parts.

Sprinkle with sesame seeds.

Bake for 20 minutes, until golden.

Over medium heat, warm a large, nonstick skillet.

Add remaining olive oil to heated pan, swirling to thinly coat bottom.

Add turkey patties to pan, sautéing, until browned and internal temperature reaches 165 degrees.

Layer each patty between two buns and serve.

Yield: 6 | Serving Size: 1 turkey patty + 2 flaxseed buns
Calories: 584   Net Carbs: 5g   Total Carbs: 21g   Fat: 42g   Protein: 33g   Fiber: 16g

Yield: 4 | Serving Size: 4 ounce (113 g) halibut fillet + ⅓ cup caprese topping

Calories: 172 Net Carbs: 1g Total Carbs: 2g Fat: 8g Protein: 24g Fiber: 1g

Lemon-Herb Halibut *with* Caprese Topping

Vibrant, simple caprese with its juicy tomatoes, creamy mozzarella and aromatic basil tops bright, herby halibut for a quick meal with layered flavors. Mild and firm halibut is my first choice, but any white fish works well, just keep an eye on the cook time.

- **2 tablespoons olive oil**

- **1 tablespoon lemon juice**

- **1 tablespoon parsley, minced**

- **1 teaspoon basil**

- **1 teaspoon garlic, minced**

- **½ teaspoon salt**

- **¼ teaspoon black pepper, divided**

- **1 pound (454 g) halibut fillet**

- **1 cup (150 g) cherry tomatoes, halved**

- **1 tablespoon extra-virgin olive oil**

- **½ cup (110 g) mozzarella pearls, halved**

- **½ teaspoon sea salt**

- **¼ cup (8 g) basil leaves**

In a small bowl, add olive oil, lemon juice, parsley, basil, garlic, salt and ⅛ teaspoon pepper, stirring, until combined.

In a large, shallow pan, arrange halibut fillet in a single layer.

Pour olive oil marinade over halibut, tossing to coat.

Cover and refrigerate for one hour.

With 30 minutes remaining...

In a small bowl, add tomatoes and extra-virgin olive oil, tossing, until well-coated.

Add mozzarella, sea salt and remaining black pepper, tossing, until combined.

Set aside.

Preheat oven to 450°F.

Line a rimmed baking sheet with parchment.

Arrange marinated halibut fillets on prepared baking sheet.

Bake until internal temperature reaches 145 degrees or desired doneness.

Add basil to tomato mixture.

Top baked fillets with caprese topping and serve immediately.

Pesto Zucchini *with* Roasted Shrimp & Parmesan

Basil and walnut pesto is the unexpected hero of this light meal. Bright and herby, while at the same time salty and rich, this sauce adds a layer of complexity to mild zucchini without overpowering the tender shrimp. Cutting the zucchini into strips adds presentation but isn't necessary. Halving lengthwise and thinly slicing is a time-saving substitute.

Please note you will need a spiralizer and food processor for this recipe.

- **3 pounds (1.4 kg) zucchini**

- **2 tablespoons olive oil, divided**

- **3 teaspoons lemon zest, divided**

- **½ teaspoon salt**

- **¼ teaspoon black pepper**

- **2 pounds (907 g) shrimp, peeled**

- **3 cups (90 g) basil**

- **⅔ cup (75 g) walnuts**

- **1 cup (40 g) Parmesan cheese, grated & divided**

- **5 tablespoons extra-virgin olive oil**

- **2 teaspoons garlic, minced**

Using a spiralizer, cut zucchini into long strips, yielding 8 cups.

Rest on a clean kitchen towel for 15 minutes.

In a small bowl, add one tablespoon olive oil, one teaspoon lemon zest, salt and pepper, stirring, until well-combined.

Add shrimp, tossing, until well-coated.

Set aside.

Preheat oven to 450°F.

Line a rimmed baking sheet with parchment.

Using a processor, add basil, walnuts, ½ cup (20 g) Parmesan, extra-virgin olive oil, garlic and remaining lemon zest, pulsing, until thick and creamy.

Set aside.

Arrange marinated shrimp on prepared baking sheet.

Roast for 8 minutes, until cooked through.

Over medium heat, warm a large, nonstick skillet.

Add remaining olive oil, swirling to thinly coat bottom.

Add spiralized zucchini, sautéing, until heated through and al dente.

Remove from heat.

Add basil pesto, tossing, until well-coated.

Top with roasted shrimp and remaining Parmesan.

Serve immediately.

Yield: 8 | Serving Size: 1 cup pesto zucchini + 4 ounce (113 g) shrimp
Calories: 348 Net Carbs: 9g Total Carbs: 12g Fat: 24g Protein: 24g Fiber: 3g

Yield: 8 | Serving Size: 2 pieces + 1 tablespoon remoulade
Calories: 259   Net Carbs: 2g   Total Carbs: 4g   Fat: 16g   Protein: 26g   Fiber: 2g

Fish Sticks *with* Spicy Remoulade

Almond flour creates a textured crust around tender, firm halibut. Paired with a spicy Louisiana-style remoulade, these fish sticks are perfect alongside a crunchy slaw for a quick summer meal. If you're looking for something a little heartier, sandwich between two flaxseed buns and top with crisp lettuce.

- ⅓ cup (80 g) mayonnaise
- 1 tablespoon chives, finely chopped
- 1 tablespoon Dijon mustard
- 1 teaspoon capers, finely chopped
- 1 teaspoon garlic, minced
- 1 teaspoon parsley, finely chopped
- 1 teaspoon Tabasco red pepper sauce
- ¼ teaspoon Worcestershire sauce
- ¼ teaspoon paprika
- ⅛ teaspoon sea salt
- ⅛ teaspoon cayenne pepper, divided
- 2 pounds (907 g) halibut fillets
- 2 eggs
- 1 cup (110 g) almond flour
- 2 teaspoons lemon zest
- 1 teaspoon garlic powder
- 1 teaspoon salt

Preheat oven to 425°F.

Line a rimmed baking sheet with parchment.

In a small bowl, add mayonnaise, chives, mustard, capers, garlic, parsley, red pepper sauce, Worcestershire sauce, paprika, sea salt and 1/16 teaspoon cayenne, stirring, until well-combined.

Cover and refrigerate.

Trim halibut into 2-ounce (56 g) pieces.

In a small bowl, whisk eggs, until frothy.

In a separate small bowl, add almond flour, lemon zest, garlic powder, salt and remaining cayenne, stirring, until combined.

Dip each piece of trimmed halibut in frothed eggs and dredge in almond flour mixture, until well-coated.

Arrange coated fish on prepared sheet in a single layer.

Bake for 15 minutes, until golden.

Serve warm with spicy remoulade.

Yield: 6 | Serving Size: 2 croquettes
Calories: 137   Net Carbs: 1g   Total Carbs: 2g   Fat: 8g   Protein: 12g   Fiber: 1g

Tuna Croquettes

Inspired by the classic French snack, these crispy, yet tender, cakes rely on baking rather than pan frying for their signature crust. With mild seasoning and simple preparation, they stand alone as a quick meal, add a protein to your favorite salad, or make a great sandwich filling.

Please note you will need a food processor for this recipe.

- **12 ounces (340 g) canned tuna in oil, drained**

- **¼ cup (60 g) mayonnaise**

- **¼ cup (20 g) Panko bread crumbs**

- **⅛ cup (6 g) chives, finely sliced**

- **1 teaspoon Dijon mustard**

- **1 teaspoon lemon juice**

- **½ teaspoon Italian seasoning**

- **¼ teaspoon garlic powder**

- **¼ teaspoon sea salt**

- **⅛ teaspoon cayenne pepper**

- **1 egg**

Preheat oven to 375°F.

Line a rimmed baking sheet with parchment.

Using a processor, pulse tuna, until finely chopped.

In a small bowl, add chopped tuna, mayonnaise, bread crumbs, chives, mustard, lemon juice, Italian seasoning, garlic powder, sea salt, cayenne and egg, stirring, until well-combined.

Using a tablespoon, divide tuna mixture into twelve parts.

Flatten and shape into patties.

Bake for 15 minutes, until golden.

Serve warm.

Yield: 4 | Serving Size: 4 ounces
Calories: 233   Net Carbs: 7g   Total Carbs: 8g   Fat: 11g   Protein: 23g   Fiber: 1g

Grilled Teriyaki Salmon

Searing salmon creates a gorgeous golden crust, serving as the perfect base for sweet, salty umami-rich teriyaki. Prepping the fillet with sesame oil, not only imparts a nutty back note, but protects the fish from drying out on the grill. For best results, grill a little shy of done, pour the glaze over the fish as soon as it comes off the heat, and let it marinate a few minutes before serving.

- 1 pound (454 g) salmon fillet
- 1 tablespoon sesame oil
- ½ teaspoon sea salt
- ¼ cup (59 ml) mirin
- 2 tablespoons sake
- 1 tablespoon ginger, minced
- 1 tablespoon reduced-sodium tamari
- 2 teaspoons garlic, minced
- 1 teaspoon brown sugar

Rub salmon with sesame oil and sprinkle with sea salt.

Set aside.

Preheat grill to 450 degrees.

Over medium heat, warm a small saucepan.

Add mirin, sake, ginger, tamari, garlic and brown sugar, stirring, until combined.

Bring glaze to a rolling boil.

Decrease heat to low, simmering for 10 minutes.

Arrange salmon skin side down on heated grill.

Close lid and cook for 6 minutes.

Remove from skin and flip fillets, searing for one minute.

Flip fillets back onto skin, cover and cook, until desired doneness.

Remove from grill, top with teriyaki glaze, and serve.

Yield: 8 | Serving Size: 1 slice

Calories: 167   Net Carbs: 3g   Total Carbs: 4g   Fat: 12g   Protein: 12g   Fiber: 1g

Crab Cheesecake

Recipes are savory memories of time and place. This slightly out of fashion dish is a return to my early entertaining days. Decadent, rich with a thick, creamy filling of crab and cheese, it's perfect as a meal with a side of lightly dressed greens or as a crowd-pleasing starter at your next gathering. If available, fresh lump crab meat has the best flavor, but canned will work as well.

Please note you will need a food processor for this recipe.

- ½ tablespoon butter
- ¼ cup (36 g) onion, finely chopped
- 1 teaspoon garlic, minced
- 1½ cups (348 g) ricotta cheese
- ¼ cup (59 ml) heavy cream
- 1 tablespoon flour
- 1 tablespoon chives, finely chopped
- 1 tablespoon parsley, finely chopped
- 1 tablespoon thyme, minced
- ½ teaspoon sea salt
- ¼ teaspoon white pepper
- 2 eggs
- 6 ounces (170 g) crab meat
- ¼ cup (12 g) scallions, finely sliced
- ¼ cup (10 g) Parmesan cheese, grated

Preheat oven to 350°F.

Coat a 9-inch springform pan with cooking spray.

Over medium heat, warm a small, nonstick skillet.

Add butter to heated pan.

Add onion and garlic, sautéing, until tender.

Remove from heat and set aside.

Using a processor, add ricotta, cream, flour, chives, parsley, thyme, sea salt and pepper, pulsing, until combined.

Add eggs, pulsing, until well-combined.

Transfer ricotta mixture to a large bowl.

Add cooked onion mixture, crab, scallions and Parmesan, stirring, until just combined.

Pour batter into prepared springform pan.

Bake for 40 minutes, until golden brown.

Remove from oven and rest for 15 minutes.

Release pan and serve.

Eggplant Manicotti *with* Sautéed Kale & Romesco

Stuffed, creamy eggplant, topped with garlicky, slightly spicy, wilted chard, and served with a smear of zippy romesco. This layered recipe is best tackled when time is no issue. It's a Sunday meal or dinner party main–beautiful, flavorful with unexpected pops of savory and spice. It can be made ahead and baked right before serving, making it a great option for entertaining.

- 2 large eggplants
- ¼ cup (59 ml) olive oil, divided
- ¼ teaspoon sea salt, divided
- ½ cup (118 ml) water
- ¼ cup (45 g) quinoa
- 1 cup (150 g) zucchini, finely chopped
- ¼ cup (20 g) red pepper, finely chopped
- 3 teaspoons garlic, minced & divided
- ⅛ cup (29 ml) low-sodium vegetable stock
- 1 tablespoon chives, minced
- ¼ teaspoon salt
- ¼ teaspoon red chili flakes
- 6 cups (150 g) chard, finely sliced
- ½ cup (140 g) romesco (see page 71)

Preheat oven to 400°F.

Line a rimmed baking sheet with parchment.

Slice eggplants lengthwise into eight 2-ounce (56 g) slices.

Arrange eggplant in a single layer on prepared sheet.

Brush eggplant with 2 tablespoons olive oil and sprinkle with ⅛ teaspoon sea salt.

Roast for 20 minutes, until golden brown and tender.

While roasting...

In a small saucepan, add water and quinoa.

Over high heat, bring quinoa mixture to a boil.

Cover and decrease heat to low, simmering for 15 minutes.

While simmering...

Over medium heat, warm a large, nonstick skillet.

Add zucchini, red pepper, one tablespoon olive oil, and two teaspoons garlic, sautéing until tender.

Add zucchini mixture, vegetable stock, chives and salt to cooked quinoa, stirring, until combined.

Recover and set aside.

Over medium heat, rewarm the large, nonstick skillet.

Add remaining olive oil, garlic, and red chili flakes, sautéing for one minute, until fragrant.

Add chard, stirring, until just wilted.

Sprinkle with remaining sea salt and set aside.

Decrease oven to 350°F.

Arrange 2 tablespoons quinoa mixture on the large, rounded end of each eggplant slice.

Roll up and place seam-side down in an oven-proof dish.

Cover with wilted chard and bake for 10 minutes, until heated through.

Serve warm with romesco.

Yield: 8 | Serving Size: 1 manicotti + 1 tablespoon romesco
Calories: 153   Net Carbs: 8g   Total Carbs: 14g   Fat: 11g   Protein: 4g   Fiber: 6g

Margherita Cauliflower Crust Pizza

Riced cauliflower makes a great textured crust. Elevated with goat cheese, Parmesan, and oregano, it's the platform for a great pizza. Crispy, slightly savory, topped with zingy sun-dried tomato marinara, fresh mozzarella, and aromatic basil—the classic margherita just became something unexpected. The key to a crispy crust begins with removing all the moisture from the grated cauliflower and finishing with a double-sided prebake.

Please note you will need a food processor for this recipe.

- **1 cup (220 g) fresh mozzarella**
- **4 cups (946 ml) water**
- **6 cups (810 g) cauliflower florets**
- **1 egg**
- **⅓ cup (40 g) goat cheese, crumbled**
- **¼ cup (10 g) Parmesan cheese, grated**
- **1 teaspoon oregano**
- **¾ cup (177 ml) sun-dried tomato marinara (see page 109)**
- **¼ cup (8 g) basil leaves**

Preheat oven to 400°F.

Line two rimmed baking sheets with parchment.

Slice mozzarella into four equal pieces.

Arrange on a clean paper towel and set aside.

Over medium heat, warm a large saucepan.

Add water, bringing to a rolling boil.

Using a processor, add cauliflower, shredding, until a rice-like texture.

Add shredded cauliflower to saucepan.

Cover pot and decrease heat to low, simmering for 5 minutes.

Drain cooked cauliflower in a fine-mesh strainer, pressing, until almost dry.

Using a clean kitchen towel, wring cauliflower, removing any excess moisture.

In a large bowl, add cooked cauliflower, egg, goat cheese, Parmesan and oregano, stirring, until well-combined.

Shape and press cauliflower mixture into a 12-inch diameter on one prepared baking sheet.

Bake for 30 minutes, until golden.

Using the parchment, flip parbaked crust to unused, prepared baking sheet.

Bake for an additional 10 minutes, until golden.

Remove from oven.

Top with sun-dried tomato marinara and sliced mozzarella.

Bake for 5 minutes, until cheese is melted.

Top with basil and serve.

Yield: 8 | Serving Size: 1 slice

Calories: 130   Net Carbs: 6g   Total Carbs: 8g   Fat: 8g   Protein: 9g   Fiber: 2g

Fresh Herb Frittata

Filled with fresh herbs and wilted chard, this frittata is a play on traditional Persian Kuku Sabzi. Quick to prepare with a fun little flip for entertainment. This dish is a great weeknight meal and even better for lunch the next day. Often served with yogurt or a squeeze of lemon, I prefer to spice it up with a smear of romesco.

• 3 cups (710 ml) water	Over medium heat, warm a large saucepan.
• 8 cups (200 g) chard, stemmed & chopped	Add water, bringing to a rolling boil.
	Decrease heat to low.
• 1 tablespoon olive oil	Add chard to saucepan and cover, steaming 2 minutes, until wilted.
• ½ cup (60 g) leeks, halved & sliced	Drain chard in a fine-mesh strainer, pressing, until almost dry.
• 2 cups (60 g) parsley, chopped	Set aside.
• 1 cup (20 g) cilantro, chopped	Over medium heat, warm a small, nonstick skillet.
• 1 cup (20 g) dill, chopped	Add olive oil to heated pan.
• 1 teaspoon salt	Add leeks, sautéing, until golden.
• ½ teaspoon pepper	Remove from heat and set aside.
• 5 eggs	In a large bowl, add drained chard, leeks, parsley, cilantro, dill, salt and pepper, stirring, until well-combined.
• 3 tablespoons butter, divided	Add eggs, one at a time, stirring in-between, until well-combined.
	Over medium heat, warm a large, nonstick skillet.
	Add 2 tablespoons butter to heated pan, stirring, until melted and bottom of pan is evenly coated.
	Add herb-egg mixture to skillet, shaping, until edges are flattened.

Rotate pan every few minutes, cooking, until bottom is brown and edges golden.

Using a spatula, lift frittata along edges, ensuring it is not stuck to pan.

Cover the skillet with a large plate.

Flip frittata onto plate.

Add remaining butter to skillet, stirring, until melted.

Transfer parcooked frittata raw side down to skillet, cooking for an additional 5 minutes, until golden.

Serve warm.

Yield: 8 | Serving Size: 1 slice

Calories: 111   Net Carbs: 3g   Total Carbs: 4g   Fat: 9g   Protein: 5g   Fiber: 1g

Yield: 6 | Serving Size: 1 crepe
Calories: 291   Net Carbs: 15g   Total Carbs: 18g   Fat: 21g   Protein: 10g   Fiber: 3g

Chestnut Crepes *with* Cheddar & Walnuts

Originating in Tuscany, ricotta-stuffed, chestnut necci date back to Medieval times. Inspired by the traditional pancake's simple recipe, sharp cheddar and walnuts replace sweet ricotta for a savory, rich crepe perfect for dinner alongside dressed greens or a bowl of soup.

- 1 cup (237 ml) water

- ½ cup (55 g) chestnut flour

- 3 eggs

- 2 tablespoons butter, divided

- ¾ cup (98 g) white cheddar, grated & divided

- ¾ cup (84 g) walnuts, chopped

In a small bowl, add water, chestnut flour and eggs, whisking, until smooth.

Rest for 10 minutes.

Over medium heat, warm a small, nonstick skillet.

Add one teaspoon butter to heated pan, stirring, until melted and bottom of pan is evenly coated.

Pour 4 tablespoons of batter into pan, tilting, until bottom of pan is evenly coated.

Cook for 2 minutes, until crepe lifts easily.

Using a spatula, flip crepe.

Arrange 2 tablespoons of cheddar on parcooked crepe.

Add 2 tablespoons walnuts to one side of crepe, fold and cook, until cheese is melted.

Repeat with remaining batter.

Serve warm.

Vegetable Lasagna

Lasagna is a classic comfort food. Warm and hearty with gooey melted cheese, it's great straight from the oven and even better the following day when flavors meld. Roasted zucchini serves as the base layer, topped with wilted chard, punchy sun-dried tomato marinara, creamy ricotta, and tangy Parmesan. Precooking the zucchini helps preserve texture, while substituting chard for more-popular spinach, keeps your sauce from becoming watery.

- 8 cups (1.2 kg) zucchini, sliced into ⅛-inch thick strips

- 1 teaspoon sea salt

- 3 tablespoons olive oil, divided

- 1 teaspoon garlic, minced

- 8 cups (200 g) chard, finely sliced

- 1½ cups (354 ml) sun-dried tomato marinara (see page 109)

- 1 cup (232 g) ricotta cheese

- 1 cup (40 g) Parmesan cheese, grated

- ½ cup (20 g) Parmesan cheese, shaved

Arrange zucchini on clean kitchen towel in a single layer.

Sprinkle with sea salt and rest for 15 minutes.

Preheat oven to 400°F.

Line a rimmed baking sheet with parchment.

Blot zucchini to remove excess moisture and transfer to prepared sheet.

Brush zucchini with 2 tablespoons olive oil.

Roast for 10 minutes, until tender.

Over medium heat, warm a large, nonstick skillet.

Add remining olive oil and garlic, sautéing for one minute, until fragrant.

Add chard, stirring, until just wilted.

Remove from heat and set aside.

In a large casserole dish, arrange ⅓ zucchini in a single bottom layer.

Spread ½ cup (118 ml) marinara over zucchini layer.

Add ½ cup (116 g) ricotta, spreading, until evenly distributed.

Add ½ cooked chard and ½ cup (20 g) grated Parmesan, spreading, until evenly distributed.

Repeat.

Arrange remaining zucchini in a final layer.

Top with remaining marinara and shaved Parmesan.

Bake uncovered for 20 minutes.

Rest for 10 minutes before serving.

Yield: 10 | Serving Size: 1 cup

Calories: 202   Net Carbs: 9g   Total Carbs: 12g   Fat: 14g   Protein: 10g   Fiber: 3g

Snacks

Life is busy and at times unpredictable; add in an active lifestyle and mealtimes can be difficult to manage. Snacking provides a balance of energy and protein when time between meals has stretched a little long or your blood sugar is feeling off.

Some days, when I find myself needing a late afternoon pick-me-up, snacks provide a healthy protein-based energy spike that doesn't interfere with my appetite for dinner.

The recipes in this section yield greater quantities, so leftovers can be easily stored and accessible to fuel your next hike, picnic, or travel.

Yield: 8 | Serving Size: 1 cup

Calories: 133   Net Carbs: 6g   Total Carbs: 11g   Fat: 9g   Protein: 5g   Fiber: 5g

Crispy Vegetable Cups *with* Peanut Sauce

Nearly a portable salad, these vegetable cups are perfect when you're on the move. Crunchy and colorful with velvety avocado, they also are a great finger food for your next gathering or picnic. Bib lettuce is delicate, so serve the peanut sauce on the side to keep the lettuce fresh and crisp.

- ⅛ cup (29 ml) reduced-sodium tamari, divided
- 1½ tablespoons rice vinegar, divided
- 1 teaspoon lemon juice
- ½ teaspoon toasted sesame oil
- ¼ teaspoon ginger, minced
- 1 cup (70 g) purple cabbage, finely shredded
- ¼ cup (70 g) peanut butter
- 2 tablespoons boiling water
- ½ teaspoon honey
- 16 bib lettuce leaves
- 1 cup (120 g) cucumber, sliced
- 1 cup (80 g) red pepper, chopped
- 1 cup (200 g) avocado, cubed
- ½ cup (38 g) carrot, grated
- ½ cup (10 g) mint leaves

In a small bowl, add one tablespoon tamari, ½ tablespoon rice vinegar, lemon juice, sesame oil and ginger, stirring, until well-combined.

Add cabbage, tossing, until evenly coated.

Set aside.

In another small bowl, add remaining tamari and rice vinegar, peanut butter, water and honey, whisking, until thick and creamy.

Set aside.

Arrange lettuce into eight cups.

Fill each with ⅛ cup (15 g) cucumber, ⅛ cup (10 g) pepper, ⅛ cup (25 g) avocado, one tablespoon marinated cabbage, one tablespoon carrot, and one tablespoon mint.

Top with one tablespoon peanut sauce and serve.

Yield: 8 | Serving Size: 1 cup vegetables + ⅛ cup fromage fort

Calories: 183   Net Carbs: 6g   Total Carbs: 10g   Fat: 13g   Protein: 9g   Fiber: 4g

Crudités *with* Fromage Fort

Fromage fort pulls together cheese remnants into a creamy, delicious spread reminiscent of fondue. Served room temperature or slightly chilled, this sauce elevates a crudités board and double-times as a fantastic spread. Savory and thick, it clings to any vegetable, especially textured brassicas.

Please note you will need a food processor for this recipe.

- 1 cup (80 g) brussels sprouts, halved

- 1 teaspoon olive oil

- 1 cup (200 g) avocado, sliced

- 1 cup (160 g) carrots, sliced

- 1 cup (120 g) cucumber, sliced

- 1 cup (100 g) green beans

- 1 cup (160 g) radish, halved

- 1 cup (80 g) Romanesco florets

- 1 cup (150 g) cherry tomatoes, halved

- 2 ounces (57 g) blue cheese, crumbled

- 2 ounces (57 g) white cheddar, grated

- 2 ounces (57 g) feta, crumbled

- 2 ounces (57 g) Parmesan cheese, grated

- ¼ cup (59 ml) dry white wine

- 2 teaspoons garlic, minced

- ¼ teaspoon black pepper

- ¹⁄₁₆ teaspoon cayenne pepper

- 1 tablespoon chives, finely chopped

~~~~~~~~~~~~~~~~~~~~~~~~~~~~~~

Preheat oven to 400°F.

Line a rimmed baking sheet with parchment.

In a small bowl, add brussels sprouts and olive oil, tossing, until well-coated.

Arrange brussels sprouts on prepared sheet.

Roast for 30 minutes, until tender.

On a large platter, arrange roasted brussels sprouts and raw vegetables for serving.

Using a processor, add blue cheese, cheddar, feta, Parmesan, white wine, garlic, black pepper and cayenne pepper, pulsing, until thick and smooth.

Top with chives and serve alongside crudités.

Yield: 6 | Serving Size: ½ cup fruit + 1 ounce (29 g) cheese
Calories: 146   Net Carbs: 9g   Total Carbs: 11g   Fat: 9g   Protein: 7g   Fiber: 2g

Fruit & Cheese Board

Bringing out the best in both flavor and balance, fruit and cheese are entirely complementary. Apples with cheddar, figs with blue: while there may be suggestions, there are no rules, except source your fruit in season whenever possible.

- **½ cup (65 g) apples, sliced**
- **½ cup (80 g) blackberries**
- **½ cup (60 g) figs, halved**
- **½ cup (80 g) grapes**
- **½ cup (70 g) raspberries**
- **½ cup (70 g) strawberries**
- **2 ounces (57 g) Brie**
- **2 ounces (57 g) blue cheese**
- **2 ounces (57 g) white cheddar**

On a large platter, arrange fruit and cheese for serving.

Serve room temperature.

Yield: 12 | Serving Size: ¼ cup
Calories: 218   Net Carbs: 11g   Total Carbs: 12g   Fat: 18g   Protein: 7g   Fiber: 1g

Rosemary Cashews

Inspired by the savory Parisian snack, these buttery rosemary cashews have a salty finish and a surprise kick thanks to a pinch of cayenne. Best served warm, they also store well in an airtight container for up to a week.

- **1 pound (453 g) cashews**
- **3 tablespoons rosemary, finely minced**
- **1 tablespoon butter, melted**
- **⅛ teaspoon cayenne pepper**
- **½ teaspoon sea salt**

Preheat oven to 325°F.

Line a rimmed baking sheet with parchment.

Arrange cashews on prepared baking sheet in a single layer.

Bake for 10 minutes.

In a small bowl, add rosemary, butter and cayenne, stirring, until combined.

Pour butter mixture over warmed nuts, tossing, until well-coated.

Rearrange in a single layer and sprinkle with sea salt.

Bake for an additional 10 minutes, until golden.

Serve warm.

Yield: 8 | Serving Size: 1 cup jicama + ¼ cup guacamole

Calories: 175   Net Carbs: 7g   Total Carbs: 19g   Fat: 11g   Protein: 3g   Fiber: 12g

Jicama *with* Guacamole

This simple, refreshing snack is perfect when the sun is high and harsh. Textured like an apple, jicama is a root vegetable with a mild, slightly sweet taste. Crunchy and chilled, it really shines when slathered with creamy, spicy guacamole. Buttery, ripe avocados are the key ingredient. If yours are on the firm side, snuggle them in a paper bag with a banana for a few days.

Please note you will need a processor for this recipe.

- ½ cup (72 g) red onion, chopped
- ¼ cup (5 g) cilantro, chopped
- 3 Hass avocados, pitted & peeled
- 2 tablespoons lime juice
- ½ teaspoon sea salt
- ⅛ teaspoon red chili flakes
- 8 cups (1.2 kg) jicama, peeled & julienned

Using a processor, add onion and cilantro, pulsing, until finely chopped.

Add avocado, lime juice and salt, pulsing, until desired consistency.

Top with chili flakes and serve alongside chilled jicama.

Yield: 6 | Serving Size: 2 crisps + ¼ cup hummus

Calories: 433   Net Carbs: 16g   Total Carbs: 25g   Fat: 33g   Protein: 16g   Fiber: 9g

Seedy Crisps & Hummus

Traditional creamy hummus seasoned with garlic, lemon, and tahini demands a crunchy, dense cracker to round out the texture and hold up to dipping. These simple almond flour crisps dotted with seeds and mildly seasoned with garlic and onion are perfect. In this recipe, nigella seeds can be substituted with flaxseeds if unavailable.

- ½ teaspoon garlic powder
- ½ teaspoon granulated onion
- ¼ teaspoon black pepper
- ¼ teaspoon salt
- 1 egg
- 1¾ cup (193 g) almond flour
- 2 tablespoons flaxseeds
- 1 tablespoon nigella seeds
- 1½ cups (345 g) hummus (see page 81)

Preheat oven to 350°F.

Line a rimless baking sheet with parchment.

In a large bowl, add garlic powder, onion, pepper, salt and egg, stirring, until well-combined.

Add almond flour, flaxseeds and nigella seeds, stirring, until well-combined.

Transfer dough to prepared sheet.

Shape dough into a rough square and cover with an additional parchment sheet.

Roll dough into a 12-by-12-inch square.

Remove top parchment and reshape edges.

Slice dough into twelve equal pieces.

Bake for 20 minutes, until golden.

Rest for 20 minutes before serving with hummus.

Yield: 12 | Serving Size: 1 cracker
Calories: 146 Net Carbs: 2g Total Carbs: 4g Fat: 12g Protein: 7g Fiber: 2g

Cheese Crackers

Grated cheddar is this recipe's shining star. Dry mustard adds a slightly tangy back note, while almond flour and flax meal add a protein boost without adding carbohydrates. If you're a fan of little orange fish crackers, this is the elevated version.

- 1½ cups (165 g) almond flour

- 1 cup (130 g) cheddar, finely grated

- ¼ cup (25 g) flaxseed meal

- ¼ teaspoon dry mustard

- ⅛ teaspoon cayenne pepper

- 2 eggs

- ⅛ teaspoon sea salt

Preheat oven to 325°F.

Line a rimless baking sheet with parchment.

In a large bowl, add almond flour, cheddar, flaxseed meal, dry mustard and pepper, stirring, until combined.

Add eggs, one at a time, stirring in-between, until well-combined and sticky.

Transfer dough to prepared sheet.

Shape dough into a rough square and cover with an additional parchment sheet.

Roll dough into a 12-by-12-inch square.

Remove top parchment and reshape edges.

Slice dough into twelve equal pieces and sprinkle with sea salt.

Bake for 25 minutes, until golden.

Rest for 20 minutes before serving.

Yield: 8 | Serving Size: 1 ball

Calories: 171   Net Carbs: 5g   Total Carbs: 8g   Fat: 14g   Protein: 6g   Fiber: 3g

Energy Balls

We all have the moment when we need a quick, protein-fueled energy boost. I keep a batch of energy balls in the refrigerator for just this occasion. Nutty, crunchy with a nice pop of cacao, these slightly sweet snacks are incredibly simple to make. I like to double the recipe as they store well refrigerated for up to a week.

- ¼ cup (70 g) almond butter
- ¼ cup (70 g) peanut butter
- 2 tablespoons cacao powder
- 2 tablespoons hemp seeds
- 2 tablespoons sunflower seeds
- 2 tablespoons water
- 1 tablespoon chia seeds
- 1 tablespoon coconut flour
- 1 tablespoon maple syrup
- ¼ cup (20 g) unsweetened coconut, shredded

In a small bowl, add almond butter, peanut butter, cacao, hemp seeds, sunflower seeds, water, chia seeds, coconut flour and maple syrup, stirring, until well-combined.

Refrigerate, uncovered for 10 minutes.

Using a tablespoon, divide dough into eight parts.

Roll and shape into balls.

In a separate small bowl, add coconut.

Roll each ball in shredded coconut.

Serve or refrigerate.

Yield: 16 | Serving Size: ¼ cup

Calories: 234 Net Carbs: 3g Total Carbs: 8g Fat: 21g Protein: 8g Fiber: 5g

Chili Lime Almonds

Inspired by Baja California, these citrus-laced, spicy almonds are insanely addicting. Try eating just one, it's not possible. For that reason, this recipe has a large yield. Once cool, transfer to a sealed glass container, a lidded mason jar works well, and store at room temperature for up to a week.

- ¼ cup (57 g) butter, melted

- 2 tablespoons Tajin seasoning

- 1 tablespoon lime juice

- 1 tablespoon paprika

- 4 cups (640 g) dry roasted almonds

- ¼ teaspoon sea salt

Preheat oven to 325°F.

Line a rimmed baking sheet with parchment.

In a large bowl, add butter, Tajin, lime juice and paprika, stirring, until well-combined.

Add almonds, tossing, until well-coated.

Arrange almonds on prepared baking sheet in a single layer and sprinkle with sea salt.

Bake for 15 minutes, until browned, but not burnt.

Rest for 10 minutes before serving.

Yield: 4 | Serving Size: 1 cup
Calories: 121 Net Carbs: 7g Total Carbs: 8g Fat: 9g Protein: 3g Fiber: 1g

Parmesan Popcorn

Before bed snacking was a tradition my mother carried over from her childhood. I'll admit some late nights or even afternoons call for a little something to take the edge off, especially if dinnertime was off schedule. Popcorn was my mom's go-to treat, she even had a special saucepan for the occasion. Light, airy with a touch of butter and salty Parmesan, this recipe is all hers.

- **1 tablespoon grapeseed oil**

- **¼ cup (60 g) corn kernels**

- **1 tablespoon butter, salted**

- **¼ cup (60 g) Parmesan cheese, finely grated**

Over medium-high heat, warm a large saucepan.

Add grapeseed oil, swirling to thinly coat bottom.

Add corn, shaking pan to distribute evenly.

Cover and cook for 3 minutes, until corn begins to pop.

Remove from heat, until silenced.

Transfer popped corn to a large bowl.

Add butter to still-warm saucepan, stirring, until melted.

Pour melted butter over popped corn.

Add Parmesan, tossing, until well-combined.

Serve immediately.

Endings

The meal is over and yet—something's missing. Perhaps it's a sense of closure, or something your palate is craving that's different from the flavors you just enjoyed?

Endings are the sunset of the meal. The moment when we celebrate the day and indulge our senses.

Dark chocolate and fruit shine in this section. The tastes are more savory than sweet, in many ways mirroring life itself.

Blueberry Tart

A play on classic blueberry pie, this tart combines a dense, almost crumbly crust, with a sweet blueberry spread. Add a scoop of fresh whipped cream for a little authenticity. When working through the recipe, don't skip the freeze, as it keeps the dough from becoming too sticky when you roll. Parchment is your best friend here and with almond flour as the base, keep an eye on your oven. Nut flours bake rapidly and quickly change from golden to burnt.

Please note you will need a processor for this recipe.

- **1 cup (120 g) almond flour**

- **5 tablespoons coconut flour**

- **½ teaspoon xanthan gum**

- **6 tablespoons salted butter, cubed**

- **¼ cup (55 g) cream cheese**

- **1 egg**

- **2 teaspoons apple cider vinegar**

- **2 cups (280 g) frozen blueberries**

- **1 tablespoon chia seeds**

- **1 teaspoon honey**

- **½ teaspoon cinnamon**

- **½ teaspoon vanilla**

Preheat oven to 375°F.

Line a rimmed baking sheet with parchment.

Using a processor, add almond flour, coconut flour and xanthan gum, pulsing, until combined.

Add butter and cream cheese, pulsing, until crumbly.

Add egg and vinegar, pulsing, until dough comes together in coarse crumbs.

Transfer dough to prepared sheet.

Shape dough into a rough round.

Freeze for 20 minutes.

While dough is setting...

Over medium-high heat, warm a small saucepan.

Add blueberries, stirring occasionally for 5 minutes, until fruit begins to break down.

Add chia seeds, honey, cinnamon and vanilla, stirring, until combined.

Remove from heat to thicken.

Top frozen dough with additional parchment sheet.

Roll dough into a ¼-inch thick round.

Remove top parchment.

Add blueberry jam mixture to center, spread, leaving a 1-inch gutter.

Fold rim over edge of filling.

Bake for 15 minutes, until golden.

Rest 20 minutes before serving.

Yield: 8 | Serving Size: 1 slice
Calories: 239   Net Carbs: 8g   Total Carbs: 13g   Fat: 20g   Protein: 5g   Fiber: 5g

Apple Croustade *with* Cheddar

A savory, minimally sweet apple tart served with sharp cheddar is a rich ending to any meal. Thinly sliced Granny Smith apples are key to a velvety, soft filling that maintains its shape. The almond flour crust demands a watchful eye as nut flours bake more rapidly than grain. If your crust goldens up with quite a few minutes left on the clock, use a pie shield to protect the edges.

Please note you will need a processor for this recipe.

- **1 cup (120 g) almond flour**

- **5 tablespoons coconut flour**

- **½ teaspoon xanthan gum**

- **7 tablespoons salted butter, cubed & divided**

- **¼ cup (55 g) cream cheese**

- **1 egg**

- **2 teaspoons apple cider vinegar**

- **4 cups (520 g) Granny Smith apples, thinly sliced**

- **1 tablespoon honey**

- **1 teaspoon cinnamon**

- **1 teaspoon vanilla**

- **8 ounces (227 g) white cheddar, sliced**

Preheat oven to 375°F.

Line a rimmed baking sheet with parchment.

Using a processor, add almond flour, coconut flour and xanthan gum, pulsing, until combined.

Add 6 tablespoons butter and cream cheese, pulsing, until crumbly.

Add egg and vinegar, pulsing, until dough comes together in coarse crumbs.

Transfer dough to prepared sheet.

Shape dough into a rough round.

Freeze for 20 minutes.

While dough is setting...

In a large bowl, add apples, honey, cinnamon and vanilla, tossing, until well-coated.

Top frozen dough with additional parchment sheet.

Roll dough into a ¼-inch thick round.

Remove top parchment.

Crimp border, creating a standing edge.

Arrange apples, working from border toward the center.

Dot filling with remaining butter.

Bake for 25 minutes, until golden.

Rest 20 minutes before serving with cheddar.

Yield: 8 | Serving Size: 1 slice + 1 ounce (28 g) cheddar

Calories: 377   Net Carbs: 13g   Total Carbs: 18g   Fat: 30g   Protein: 12g   Fiber: 5g

Yield: 8 | Serving Size: 1 cup berries + ¼ cup whipped cream

Calories: 164   Net Carbs: 10g   Total Carbs: 15g   Fat: 11g   Protein: 2g   Fiber: 5g

Berries *with* Whipped Cream

Simple, but so delicious. Pillowy, cloud-like whipped cream dotted with juicy, sweet blackberries, raspberries and strawberries. This dessert is best when seasonal berries are at their peak. The secret to voluminous whipped cream is a chilled, preferably metal, bowl. I like to pop mine in the freezer about 30 minutes beforehand.

Please note you will need an electric mixer for this recipe.

- **1 cup (237 ml) heavy cream, chilled**

- **2 tablespoons powdered sugar**

- **1 teaspoon vanilla**

- **2 cups (320 g) blackberries**

- **2 cups (280 g) raspberries**

- **4 cups (568 g) strawberries, halved**

In a large, chilled bowl, add heavy cream, sugar and vanilla.

Using an electric mixer, whip on medium-high, until soft peaks form.

Refrigerate.

In a large bowl, add blackberries, raspberries and strawberries, mixing, until combined.

Divide berries into eight cups.

Top each with 4 tablespoons chilled whipped cream and serve immediately.

Yield: 8 | Serving Size: 1 pear half + ½ tablespoon dukkah

Calories: 114   Net Carbs: 15g   Total Carbs: 19g   Fat: 5g   Protein: 2g   Fiber: 4g

Cider Poached Pears *with* Dukkah

Fragrant autumnal spices combine with sweet apple cider in a slow-cook marinade for velvety, ripe pears. Dukkah is an Egyptian blend of seeds, nuts and spices that complements the poached fruit perfectly with its nutty, aromatic crunch. Toasting is an important step for unlocking unexpected flavors, but make sure to kill the heat once slightly golden to ensure the seeds and nuts don't burn and turn bitter.

Please note you will need a processor for this recipe.

- **⅛ cup (20 g) sesame seeds**
- **¼ cup (40 g) hazelnuts**
- **⅛ cup (17 g) pistachio meats**
- **1½ teaspoons cinnamon, divided**
- **⅛ teaspoon allspice**
- **⅛ teaspoon cardamon**
- **⅜ teaspoon cloves, divided**
- **⅛ teaspoon coriander**
- **2 cups (473 ml) apple cider**
- **½ teaspoon ginger**
- **¼ teaspoon nutmeg**
- **4 ripe Bosc pears, peeled & halved**

Over medium heat, warm a small skillet.

Add sesame seeds, stirring, until toasted and golden.

Transfer toasted seeds to a small bowl.

Rewarm skillet.

Add hazelnuts, stirring, until golden and fragrant.

Using a processor, add toasted hazelnuts and pistachios, pulsing, until coarsely chopped.

Add chopped nuts, ½ teaspoon cinnamon, allspice, cardamon, ⅛ teaspoon cloves and coriander to sesame seeds, stirring, until combined.

Set aside.

Over medium-high heat, warm a large saucepan.

Add cider, remaining cinnamon and cloves, ginger and nutmeg, stirring, until combined.

Bring cider mixture to a rolling boil.

Add pear halves.

Decrease heat to low and cover, simmering for 20 minutes, until pears are tender.

Remove from cider, top each pear with ½ tablespoon dukkah and serve.

Yield: 8 | **Serving Size: ½ cup oranges + 1 tablespoon dates**

Calories: 67   Net Carbs: 14g   Total Carbs: 17g   Fat: 1g   Protein: 1g   Fiber: 3g

Citrus & Dates

Southern California's hot, sunny days and dry, cool nights produce exceptional citrus. In addition, the state's Coachella Valley is a prolific source of chewy, caramel-like medjool dates. The winter season brings an abundance of both. This simple dessert is a little California sun during the time of the year when we all could benefit from a natural dose of vitamin C.

- **2 cups (350 g) blood oranges, peeled & sliced**

- **2 cups (350 g) navel oranges, peeled & sliced**

- **½ cup (110 g) medjool dates, pitted & thinly sliced**

On a large platter, arrange oranges and dates for serving.

Serve at room temperature.

Chocolate Peanut Butter Shortbread

A house favorite—to be honest they should come with a warning sign, they are that good. Slightly crumbly shortbread, topped with creamy, naturally sweet peanut butter, coated in a layer of rich, decadent dark chocolate. Quick setting the melted chocolate in the freezer is an important step to ensure beautiful, crisp edges. While these treats can be served at room temperature, I think they are best chilled.

Please note you will need a processor for this recipe.

- 1 cup (120 g) almond flour

- ½ cup (56 g) coconut flour

- ⅓ cup (76 g) butter, room temperature

- 1½ tablespoons maple syrup

- 1 teaspoon vanilla

- ⅛ teaspoon salt

- 1 cup (280 g) peanut butter, warmed

- 3 cups (710 ml) water

- 6 ounces (170 g) 85% dark chocolate, chopped

- 1 tablespoon coconut oil

- ⅛ teaspoon espresso

- ¼ teaspoon sea salt

Preheat oven to 325°F.

Line an 8-inch square baking pan with parchment.

Using a processor, add almond flour, coconut flour, butter, maple syrup, vanilla and salt, pulsing, until dough forms.

Transfer dough to prepared pan.

Press into a crust, until dough forms an even layer to the edges.

Bake for 15 minutes, until golden.

Spread peanut butter in a thin layer over warm crust.

Set aside.

Over medium heat, warm a large saucepan.

Add water and simmer.

Fit a small glass bowl inside saucepan, creating a double boiler.

Decrease heat, ensuring water does not splash into the bowl.

Add chocolate, coconut oil and espresso to bowl, stirring occasionally, until melted and combined.

Pour melted chocolate mixture over peanut butter layer, spreading, until evenly distributed.

Freeze for 5 minutes.

Top with sea salt, retuning to freezer for 15 minutes, until set.

Using the parchment, remove shortbread from baking pan.

Slice shortbread into 16 squares.

Serve or store refrigerated.

Yield: 16 | Serving Size: 1 bar

Calories: 255   Net Carbs: 10g   Total Carbs: 14g   Fat: 21g   Protein: 6g   Fiber: 4g

Chocolate Hazelnut Truffles

From spreads to candies, dark chocolate and hazelnuts have a long history together. This is our play on the classic combination. Rich, velvety chocolate truffles enjoy a crunchy, nutty finish in this simple, albeit messy, recipe. Dusting your hands in cacao powder and working quickly creates a beautiful truffle, while storing refrigerated until serving maintains their integrity.

Please note you will need a processor for this recipe.

- **9 ounces (255 g) 85% dark chocolate, finely chopped**

- **1 tablespoon butter, room temperature**

- **⅔ cup (158 ml) heavy cream**

- **1 teaspoon vanilla**

- **1 cup (160 g) blanched hazelnuts**

- **1 teaspoon cacao powder**

Line an 8-inch square baking pan with parchment.

In a small, heatproof bowl, add chocolate and butter.

Set aside.

Over medium heat, warm a small saucepan.

Add heavy cream, stirring, until simmering.

Pour heated cream over chocolate and butter.

Rest until chocolate is melted.

Add vanilla to melted chocolate mixture, stirring gently, until smooth.

Transfer to baking pan.

Cover surface with plastic wrap.

Refrigerate for 2 hours.

While chilling...

Over medium heat, warm a small skillet.

Add hazelnuts, stirring, until golden and fragrant.

Using a processor, add toasted hazelnuts, pulsing, until chopped.

Transfer chopped nuts to a small bowl.

Set aside.

Remove chocolate mixture from refrigerator.

Using a tablespoon, divide into 24 parts.

Lightly dust hands with cacao powder, rolling each part into a ball.

Roll each ball in toasted hazelnuts.

Cover and refrigerate for one hour before serving.

Yield: 24 | Serving Size: 1 ball

Calories: 115   Net Carbs: 4g   Total Carbs: 6g   Fat: 10g   Protein: 2g   Fiber: 2g

Yield: 8 | Serving Size: 1 ounce (28 g)

Calories: 150   Net Carbs: 9g   Total Carbs: 12g   Fat: 12g   Protein: 3g   Fiber: 3g

Raspberry Almond Bark

Chocolate and raspberries are better together than individually. Both have merit, but combined they are exceptional. Smooth, rich dark chocolate is even better with a slight crunch. Finely chopped almonds provide texture with the added bonus of enhancing the chocolate's flavor. All said, this bark is nothing short of delicious.

- **3 cups (710 ml) water**

- **5 ounces (142 g) 85% dark chocolate, finely chopped**

- **½ teaspoon coconut oil**

- **½ cup (80 g) almonds, finely chopped**

- **2 teaspoons freeze-dried raspberry powder**

Line a rimmed baking sheet with parchment.

Over medium heat, warm a large saucepan.

Add water and simmer.

Fit a small glass bowl inside saucepan, creating a double boiler.

Decrease heat, ensuring water does not splash into the bowl.

Add chocolate and coconut oil, stirring occasionally, until melted and combined.

Add chopped almonds, stirring, until combined.

Transfer to prepared sheet and spread in an even layer.

Sprinkle with dried raspberry powder.

Freeze for 10 minutes.

Remove from freezer and rest at room temperature for one hour.

Cut into 1-ounce or 2 tablespoon-sized pieces.

Serve or store refrigerated.

Yield: 12 | Serving Size: 1 bonbon
Calories: 115   Net Carbs: 6g   Total Carbs: 8g   Fat: 10g   Protein: 2g   Fiber: 2g

Pistachio Bonbons

Rich, dark chocolate envelopes sweet, slightly salty pistachio butter. I'll admit bonbon is a loose description of this candy, as it really depends on the mold you use, but the traditional French description of a hard chocolate shell filled with a soft filling holds true. I leave the signature decoration up to you.

Please note you will need a 12-cavity silicone candy mold for this recipe.

- **3 cups (710 ml) water**

- **6 ounces (170 g) 85% dark chocolate, finely chopped**

- **½ teaspoon coconut oil**

- **¼ cup (80 g) pistachio butter (see page 67)**

Place candy mold on a rimmed baking sheet lined with parchment.

Over medium heat, warm a large saucepan.

Add water and simmer.

Fit a small glass bowl inside saucepan, creating a double boiler.

Decrease heat, ensuring water does not splash into the bowl.

Add chocolate and coconut oil, stirring occasionally, until melted and combined.

Using a teaspoon, pour melted chocolate mixture into the cavities of the silicone candy mold, until each is partially filled.

Using a silicone pastry brush, spread chocolate within each cavity, until sides are well-coated.

Freeze for 5 minutes.

Remove from freezer and add one teaspoon pistachio butter to each cavity.

Using a teaspoon, top each cavity with remaining chocolate, until all twelve are filled.

Freeze for 10 minutes, until set.

Remove candy from mold.

Serve or store refrigerated.

Yield: 12 | Serving Size: 1 piece
Calories: 108   Net Carbs: 6g   Total Carbs: 8g   Fat: 9g   Protein: 2g   Fiber: 2g

Peanut Butter Cups

Timeless and classic. Dark chocolate peanut butter cups topped with a slight sprinkle of coarse sea salt. A silicone pastry brush is a great tool for coating the sides of the mold with melted chocolate, ensuring you take your first nibble of creamy peanut butter completely surrounded in rich, decadent goodness.

Please note you will need a 12-cavity silicone candy mold for this recipe.

- **3 cups (710 ml) water**

- **6 ounces (170 g) 85% dark chocolate, finely chopped**

- **½ teaspoon coconut oil**

- **¼ cup (70 g) peanut butter**

- **⅛ teaspoon sea salt**

Place candy mold on a rimmed baking sheet lined with parchment.

Over medium heat, warm a large saucepan.

Add water and simmer.

Fit a small glass bowl inside saucepan, creating a double boiler.

Decrease heat, ensuring water does not splash into the bowl.

Add chocolate and coconut oil, stirring occasionally, until melted and combined.

Using a teaspoon, pour melted chocolate mixture into the cavities of the silicone candy mold, until each is partially filled.

Using a silicone pastry brush, spread chocolate within each cavity, until sides are well-coated.

Freeze for 5 minutes.

Remove from freezer and add one teaspoon peanut butter to each cavity.

Using a teaspoon, top each cavity with remaining chocolate, until all twelve are filled.

Sprinkle with sea salt.

Freeze for 10 minutes, until set.

Remove candy from mold.

Serve or store refrigerated.

Yield: 12 | Serving Size: 1 piece
Calories: 253   Net Carbs: 9g   Total Carbs: 13g   Fat: 23g   Protein: 3g   Fiber: 4g

Chocolate Coconut Bars

Coconut macaroons inspired these mounds of unsweetened coconut dipped in rich, velvety dark chocolate. Coconut milk powder is the secret ingredient binding the coconut flakes to create a slightly creamy filling. Freezing the bars before dipping ensures they hold together nicely, and I recommend storing refrigerated until serving.

- ½ cup (64 g) coconut milk powder

- 2 tablespoons butter, melted

- 2 tablespoons boiling water

- ⅛ teaspoon salt

- 2 cups (160 g) shredded, unsweetened coconut

- 3 cups (710 ml) water

- 6 ounces (170 g) 85% dark chocolate, finely chopped

- ½ teaspoon coconut oil

Line a rimless baking sheet with parchment.

In a large bowl, add coconut milk powder, butter, boiling water and salt, stirring, until well-combined.

Add coconut, stirring, until well-combined.

Using a tablespoon, divide coconut mixture into twelve parts.

Shape each into a rectangle and place on prepared sheet.

Freeze for 30 minutes, until firm.

Over medium heat, warm a large saucepan.

Add water and simmer.

Fit a small glass bowl inside saucepan, creating a double boiler.

Decrease heat, ensuring water does not splash into the bowl.

Add chocolate and coconut oil, stirring occasionally, until melted and combined.

Dip each frozen coconut bar in melted chocolate and return to baking sheet.

Freeze for 10 minutes, until set.

Remove from freezer.

Serve or store refrigerated.

Yield: 8 | Serving Size: ¼ cup

Calories: 130   Net Carbs: 10g   Total Carbs: 12g   Fat: 9g   Protein: 3g   Fiber: 2g

Chocolat Chaud

When time permits, this is the nourishing and decadent treat I enjoy to gently close the day. Inspired by the classic Parisian beverage, warm and rich chocolat chaud is the perfect balance of bitter and sweet. Simply melted chocolate and milk, it is best made from the highest-quality dark chocolate you can endure melting down.

- **3 cups (710 ml) water**

- **5 ounces (142 g) 85% dark chocolate, finely chopped**

- **2 cups (473 ml) whole milk**

Over medium heat, warm a large saucepan.

Add water and simmer.

Fit a small glass bowl inside saucepan, creating a double boiler.

Decrease heat, ensuring water does not splash into the bowl.

Add chocolate, stirring occasionally, until melted.

Remove from heat.

Over medium-low heat, warm a small saucepan.

Add milk, whisking, until heated through.

Add melted chocolate, whisking for 5 minutes, until thickened.

Serve immediately.

Oven Settings

Simply stated, all ovens are different. For reference, the temperatures in this book are based on a European (fan-assisted) convection oven. If you are using a different option, cook times might vary slightly.

OVEN TEMPERATURES

Farenheit (F)	Celsius (C) (approximate)
200	95
250	120
300	150
325	165
350	180
375	190
400	200
425	220
450	230

Thank you.

My deepest gratitude to everyone who has supported this effort as nothing means more than your words of encouragement and knowing my recipes have been invited into your kitchen.

There are many people who specifically inspired, contributed, and helped bring this book to life. To each of you, I am forever indebted.

Jennifer Newens, your unwavering belief in this story and fearless initial leap started the journey, while your editorial encouragement kept it moving forward.

Lindsy Richards, your natural aesthetic and innate ability to capture a moment elevated the backdrop of this otherwise placeless narrative.

Knowing your farmer is a profound privilege, to the extended Chino's family for your endless inspiration, humbling work ethic, farm to table genius and fresh-picked bounty that filled not only the pages of this book, but my daily table.

Dr. Cheryl Anderson for your informative, yet eloquent foreword, as well as your beautiful mix of validation and optimism.

Hugo Villabona for letting my vision inspire this book. Megan Werner for your patience and creativity, Robin Miller, Elina Diaz, and the entire team at Mango Publishing for not only your support and expertise but giving me the opportunity to share this story with the world.

Vanessa Wertheim's behind the scenes cheerleading and Michelle Addy's legal red pen both pushed this project well beyond anything in my skillset. While my dearest pen pal, June Emmert has graciously written three decades of perfectly scripted words of encouragement. I'm truly grateful.

To my immediate family, I hold you closest to my heart. Lucy, the best prep chef, ingredient hunter, taste tester, recipe developer, proofreader, and hand model anyone could ask for. Marc for starting it all with the three b's of bliss. Since then, your dishwashing skills and endless tech support have never failed me. Mom, from you I learned to stir and sauté and, Dad, you created my first kitchen sandbox. Finally Mia, for without you, none of this would have been possible. Be well.

Contributors

FOREWORD AUTHOR - CHERYL A. M. ANDERSON, PHD, MPH, MS, FAHA

Dr. Cheryl Anderson is Professor and Founding Dean of the University of California San Diego Herbert Wertheim School of Public Health and Human Longevity Science, with a joint appointment in the Department of Medicine Division of Nephrology and Hypertension. She holds the Hood Family Endowed Dean's Chair in Public Health and serves as Director of the UC San Diego Center of Excellence in Health Promotion and Equity.

Dr. Anderson is a cardiovascular disease epidemiologist whose research focuses on the role of nutrition in the prevention of cardiovascular diseases and chronic kidney disease. This body of research aims is related to diabetes management, healthy diet, physical activity, weight management, blood pressure control, cholesterol management, smoking cessation, and sleep. Her work on dietary sodium, blood pressure, and cardiovascular health has influenced behavioral strategies that have been implemented across the globe for the prevention and management of heart diseases and chronic kidney disease.

Dr. Anderson has served on the prestigious National Academy of Medicine's Food and Nutrition Board and the US Dietary Guidelines Advisory Committee – efforts that influence public health policies about food intake and nutrition status of millions of Americans. She is a Fellow of the American Heart Association, the immediate past Chair of the American Heart Association's Epidemiology and Prevention Council, and the current Chair of the American Heart Association's Council Operations Committee. She also serves as a deputy editor for Diabetes Care and is on the editorial board for Nutrition Reviews and Circulation.

In recognition of her career accomplishments, she was elected to the National Academy of Medicine in 2016.

LIFESTYLE PHOTOGRAPHER - LINDSY RICHARDS

California native Lindsy Richards has honed her holistic and organic style behind the lens of her Nikon. After graduating from the University of Colorado, she spent the next two decades working with fashion brands and action sports figures. With camera in hand, Lindsy united her passion of natural beauty and photography in 2011, founding Flora Aura designs. The online platform showcases handcrafted floral wearables and aesthetic imagery from her hometown of Encinitas, California where she lives with her husband and two children.

CHINO FARM

Chino Nojo is a family-owned farm, established in 1946 on 50 acres of river-bottom land in Rancho Santa Fe, California. In 1975, Chino Farm, which specializes in heirloom varieties of fruits and vegetables, gained widespread recognition when Alice Waters began using their vegetables at her world-renowned restaurant, Chez Panisse. Today, Chino's corn, green beans, watermelon, berries, and other delicious and rare items can be found on restaurant menus all over Southern California. The stand, open year-round, is a mainstay for food lovers in the area, and a ritual stop for foodies visiting San Diego. Continuing the family's quest for never-ending flavor, Aisu Creamery opened in 2022, featuring hand-made ice cream showcasing the farm's seasonal ingredients captured at peak ripeness.

About the Author

Jennifer Shun is a writer, skilled home cook, and mother of a daughter living with Type 1 diabetes. She shares her recipe development, food styling and photography passions on her diabetic lifestyle blog forgoodmeasure. com, as well as her for.good.measure Instagram account. She is also the author of the novel-in-stories *We Once Had Wings*. Jennifer lives with her husband, daughters, and black cat in southern California. Guaranteed she's writing something with a #2 Ticonderoga as you read this, while a Dutch oven simmers.

Index

W

X

Y

Z

Mango Publishing, established in 2014, publishes an eclectic list of books by diverse authors—both new and established voices—on topics ranging from business, personal growth, women's empowerment, LGBTQ+ studies, health, and spirituality to history, popular culture, time management, decluttering, lifestyle, mental wellness, aging, and sustainable living. We were named 2019 *and* 2020's #1 fastest growing independent publisher by *Publishers Weekly*. Our success is driven by our main goal, which is to publish high-quality books that will entertain readers as well as make a positive difference in their lives.

Our readers are our most important resource; we value your input, suggestions, and ideas. We'd love to hear from you—after all, we are publishing books for you!

Please stay in touch with us and follow us at:

Facebook: Mango Publishing

Twitter: @MangoPublishing

Instagram: @MangoPublishing

LinkedIn: Mango Publishing

Pinterest: Mango Publishing

Newsletter: mangopublishinggroup.com/newsletter

Join us on Mango's journey to reinvent publishing, one book at a time.